Native Soil

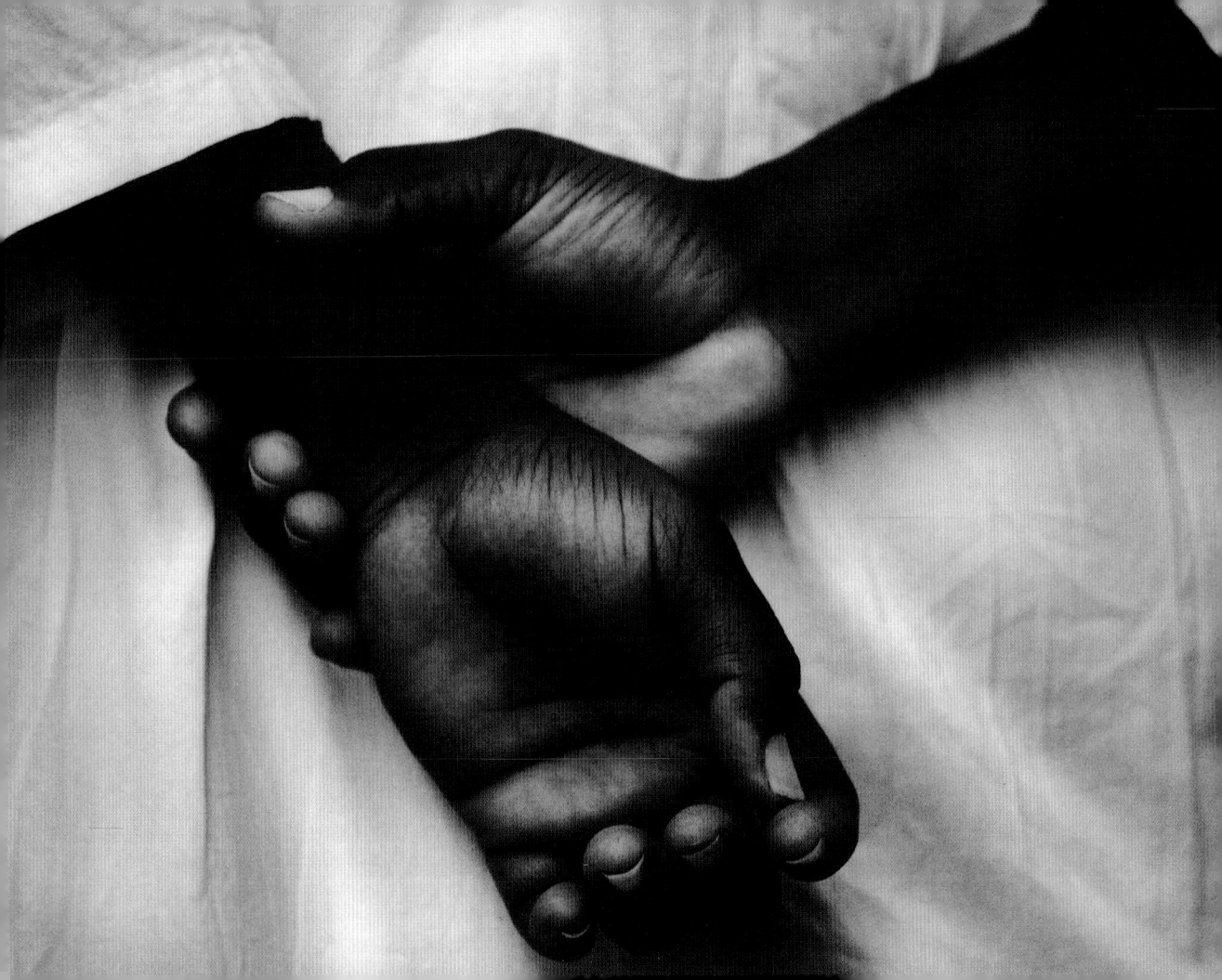

Native Soil

Photographs by Jack Spencer

Introduction by Ellen Douglas

Louisiana State University Press   Baton Rouge

Copyright © 1999 by Jack Spencer
Introduction © 1999 by Louisiana State University Press
All rights reserved
Manufactured in Hong Kong
First printing
08 07 06 05 04 03 02 01 00 99
5 4 3 2 1

Designer: Michele Myatt Quinn
Typeface: Goudy
Printer and binder: C&C Offset Printing Co., Ltd.

Library of Congress Cataloging-in-Publication Data
Spencer, Jack.
    Native Soil: images of the South / photographs by Jack Spencer; introduction by Ellen Douglas.
      p.   cm.
    ISBN 0-8071-2475-3 (cl. : alk. paper)
    1. Southern States Pictorial works. 2. Southern States—Social life and customs Pictorial works. 3. Southern States—Biography Pictorial works. I. Title.
F210.S72   1999   99-27319
975'.043'0222—dc21   CIP

The paper in this book meets the guidelines for permanence and durability of the Committee on Production Guidelines for Book Longevity of the Council on Library Resources. ∞

Title-spread photograph: Two Hands. 1995, Moon Lake, Miss.
Photograph opposite Afterword: Alex's Hands. 1990, England Ark.

To Dot, Linda, Polly, Pirl, and Mary Lou

Beginning with *Sartoris* I discovered that my own little postage stamp of native soil was worth writing about and that I would never live long enough to exhaust it . . .

—William Faulkner

Contents

Introduction by Ellen Douglas	1
Native Soil	5
Afterword and Acknowledgments	157

Introduction

ELLEN DOUGLAS

Jack Spencer's photographs—the faces, the stances, the staged presences—invite me first to think about stories, and indeed, Spencer has described his work as akin to short stories. The images, he has said, imply an occurrence, an event, behind each two-dimensional photograph. I would go further and say that his pictures are art works in the same way that stories or songs or sculptures are art works. What the photographer has done in the dark room to form his finished picture ranks at the same level of intensification as his choice of frame and image at the moment of snapping the shutter. Everything (at least to my untutored eye) seems as planned—as *made*—as a novel or a short story or a painting or a piece of music.

I pick out two or three of these images. I could begin with "Gladys and Her Mother Behind Clothesline." The figures and faces are veiled by a translucent sheet, not a bedsheet, surely, for the light glimmers through as if through a sheet of visquine. We see nothing of either figure except that they are so close as to seem to be clinging to each other. But of course, below the sheet, grounded in earth, we see the two women's feet, Gladys's outgrown tennis shoes, her bare heels and, to one side, the seatless chair, the trash-littered ground and broken screen door—the material world, rendered in sharp focus. The women behind the sheet—their story is all potentiality, all mystery, their world all harsh reality. The picture opens doors to imaginable possibilities—and perhaps closes others, for we cannot see their faces.

And then, "Mr. Bihm and Sons," the sons not beside him but receding into the shadows. One son smiles: He has managed to survive his father's powerful personality. The other? The other recedes even farther, fades back. We can't quite see his eyes. Is his stance threatening? Wounded? In the foreground is that extraordinary, powerful old man, the very hairs of his mustache, the hair springing up from his scalp expressing his strength, and yet—perhaps—on second look, his benevolence, too. Is the benevolence real or a mask? Only a story would tell us, and the best story might leave us still in doubt.

When I began to write, I used the word "staged"

advisedly. These pictures are arranged. They are far different from Cartier-Bresson's, for example, of whom critic John Berger wrote, "The photographic moment is an instant, a fraction of a second, and he stalks that instant as if it were a wild animal." Or from Paul Strand's, of whom the same critic writes, "Some would say his photographs fail, for they remain *details* [italics mine] of what they have been taken from: they never become independent images. Nature . . . is intransigent to art." Or from Eudora Welty's. She, like Cartier-Bresson, clicks on the moment—on the canted hip, the framed gesture that reveals weariness, joy, sexuality, power, or love.

For Spencer, it seems to me, nature is not intransigent to art. That is, he successfully calls forth his art from nature. Welty wrote of her story "A Worn Path": "One day I saw a solitary old woman like Phoenix. She was walking. I saw her at middle distance, in a winter country landscape, and watched her slowly make her way across my line of vision. That sight of her made me write the story." She speaks here of an image that might have become a photograph, but that instead, wrested from nature, became a story. Just so, Spencer wrests his picture of Willie Mae and the milo field from nature. He begins, of course, by choosing and recording an image, as Welty chose her glimpse of Phoenix, or as a painter chooses his subject; but then there is the darkroom work—the attention to and subtle altering of light and darkness, frame and image, as if in the staging and in the darkroom, the artist, through his manipulations, struggles to break free of the coincidental, the contingent. Spencer has said, in fact, "I sometimes spend days trying to find out what a negative is saying to me."

Herbert Marcuse calls art "the great refusal." These photographs seem to me to be a conscious wresting of images out of the world-as-it-is—contingency—and into the category of "the great refusal," the symbolic form that reveals, *re*-forms, intensifies, illumines, the world-as-it-is. There lies the story.

But such an intent also requires the photographer to permit mystery to exist, to endure the pain of unresolved mystery—and these pictures are nothing if not mysterious. Keats called the capacity of the artist to be ". . . in uncertainties, doubts, without any irritable reaching after fact and reason," *negative capability*, and Jack Spencer's work is a witness to that quality. These are mysterious pictures. They exist, it seems to me, in a human time and space between "Merit Creek," which strikes me as the sparkling, pristine, watery world-as-it-was-before-we-came, between that time and the time of the church ruin or of the empty swinging tires (moved not by human hands but by a faint subsiding breeze), or of the magnificent water-scape of Lake Pontchartrain, images, all of which might be pictures of the world-as-it-will-be after we're gone. In the in-between we see mysterious people pursuing their lives.

In "Dawn Fire," a man on whose almost obscured face I see what seems to me a look of wonder or expectation confronts us across a trinity of spiraling flames. His figure is caught in a halo of smoke. Behind him is what appears to be part of a rusted or dismembered tractor or truck. On whom might this fire be visited? Is it under his control?

Or Cooter, his back to us, makes his way along an uphill road. What lies over the hill, in the darkness at the road's turning?

Kate stands alone in the night street, her face lifted, behind her a burst of light, but on her face a look of stern reservation. Her story is *her* secret. But what story do "Patriot No. 1" and "Patriot No. 2" invite us to invent, one with its starred, furled flag set over against the man's half-veiled face, and the other with its look of—what? Anger? Revulsion?

And the animals. What about the animals? The four

white horses shining against the enveloping darkness. The rooster, every feather articulated beneath his curved beak and powerful comb and staring eye. (Is he really *Jimmie's* rooster—Jimmie, who fades into the background like a figure made of mist? Or is it the other way around? Is Jimmie the rooster's boy?) The Dominicker, less threatening than the rooster, but far more solid than the cropped figure that holds her with dissolving hands. And finally, that terrible dead fish held by a headless figure—a dead fish that seems, with its flexed tail and glittering skin, more alive than the fisherman.

Are the animals waiting for us to go?

In part this is a surreal world, a world of distances and screens and veils and silences and the opening and closing of doors. Cooter stands foursquare, deliberately obscuring his own face behind a sheet of ground glass, held in his precisely articulated hands, his head framed twice, once by the veil of glass and again by the weathered wall behind him. In "Amorous Window" crossed mullions slash through the yearning sexually charged faces of a man and a woman. This is a photograph of a photograph that sits behind a window, letters of an old sign—CURL—tumbling downward toward the figures. All is falling apart inside the frame, the wall behind the figures pocked and cracked, the sign below them an undecipherable fading message; and in front of them, containing them, the miraculously visible reticulations of a window screen.

Most curious of all, perhaps, most skewed to our conventional expectations, is "Reverend Stokes's Baptismal Pool." Reverend Stokes is seated on the edge of a square, vat-like concrete container, in front of him a batttered vase of flowers. Huge staggering letters are painted on the wall of the pool, reading I BELIEVE JESUS LIVED LIKE THEY SAID. Trickles of paint drip down from the letters. Behind the pool there is a pile of twentieth-century detritus: broken metal chairs, a car seat, part of a wrecked trailer. Reverend Stokes is in profile. He appears to be profoundly indifferent to the scene and to the photographer's presence.

Pictures are by definition silent, are they not? But these two—although words are a part of them, still we are baffled, as we are by the suggestion of unheard music in "Cooter in the Corn with Horn," where lush, curving leaves rhythmically repeat and repeat the curving shapes of the horn, and Cooter might be ready to conduct the orchestra.

Perhaps we should ask, too, for the photographer's story. He, after all, is the one who chooses the images, who goes into the dark room and manipulates light and shadow, who crops and frames. He chose to obscure Gladys and her mother behind the veil of a hanging plastic sheet. He expressed his own stoic loneliness in landscapes and water-scapes empty of human figures, his respect for human strength and endurance in the faces of Gussie and Willie Mae and Eugene and Mr. Will and Alex and M. L.

There are other pictures that seem to me to express—whether deliberately or by happenstance—his preoccupations, or to throw a mysterious light on his life-as-an-artist, some as if drifting up from that reservoir of the unconscious where all art begins, others like dreams or remembered joy. There is the photograph of the three boys riding their bicycles out of the everyday world into an imagined—a dreamed—adventure. There is the swimmer, distorted by water into a monster emerging from nightmare, and there is that wonderful joyous image of the boy, bathed in light, performing for his watching friends and family, swinging far out over the pond, daring to swing higher, ready to let go, to dive deep into the water with its warm surface, its veins of cool darkness.

And there is the man sleeping in a pool, who is perhaps dreaming this book.

Native Soil

Willie Mae and the Milo Field. 1998, Marks, Miss.

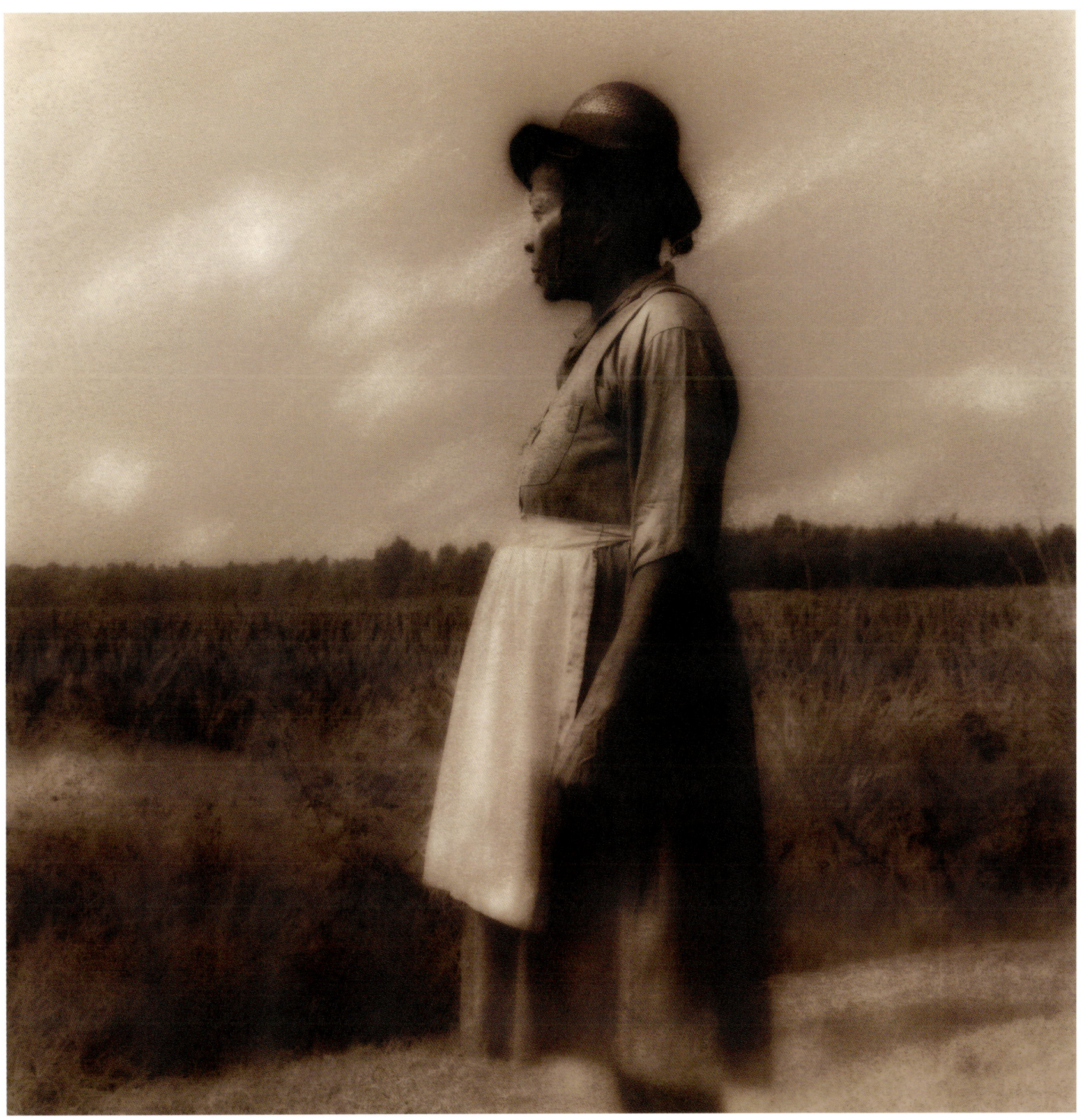

Gladys and Her Mother Behind Clothesline. 1998, Cove City, S.C.

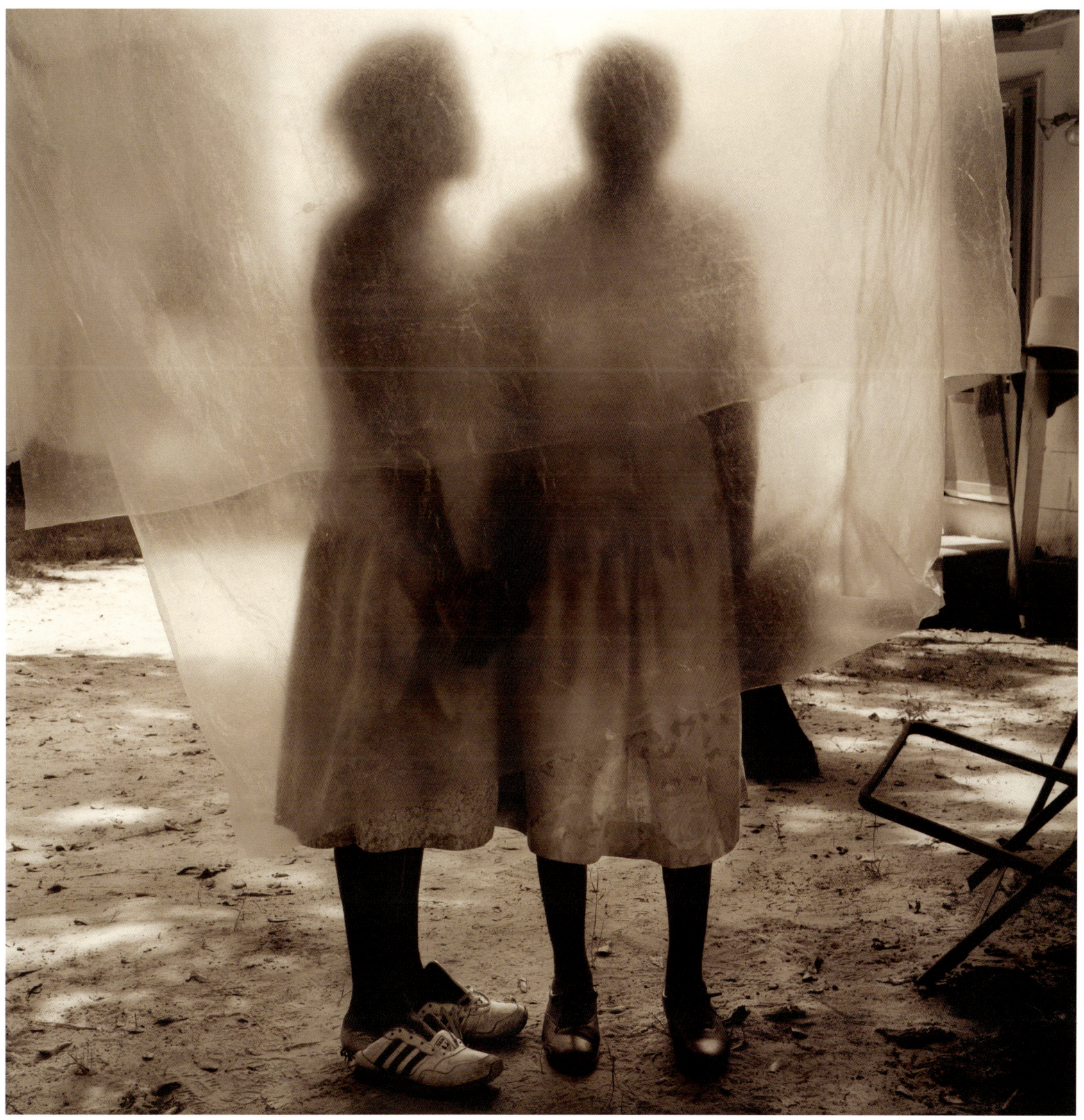

Gussie's Magnolia. 1997, LaGrange, Tenn.

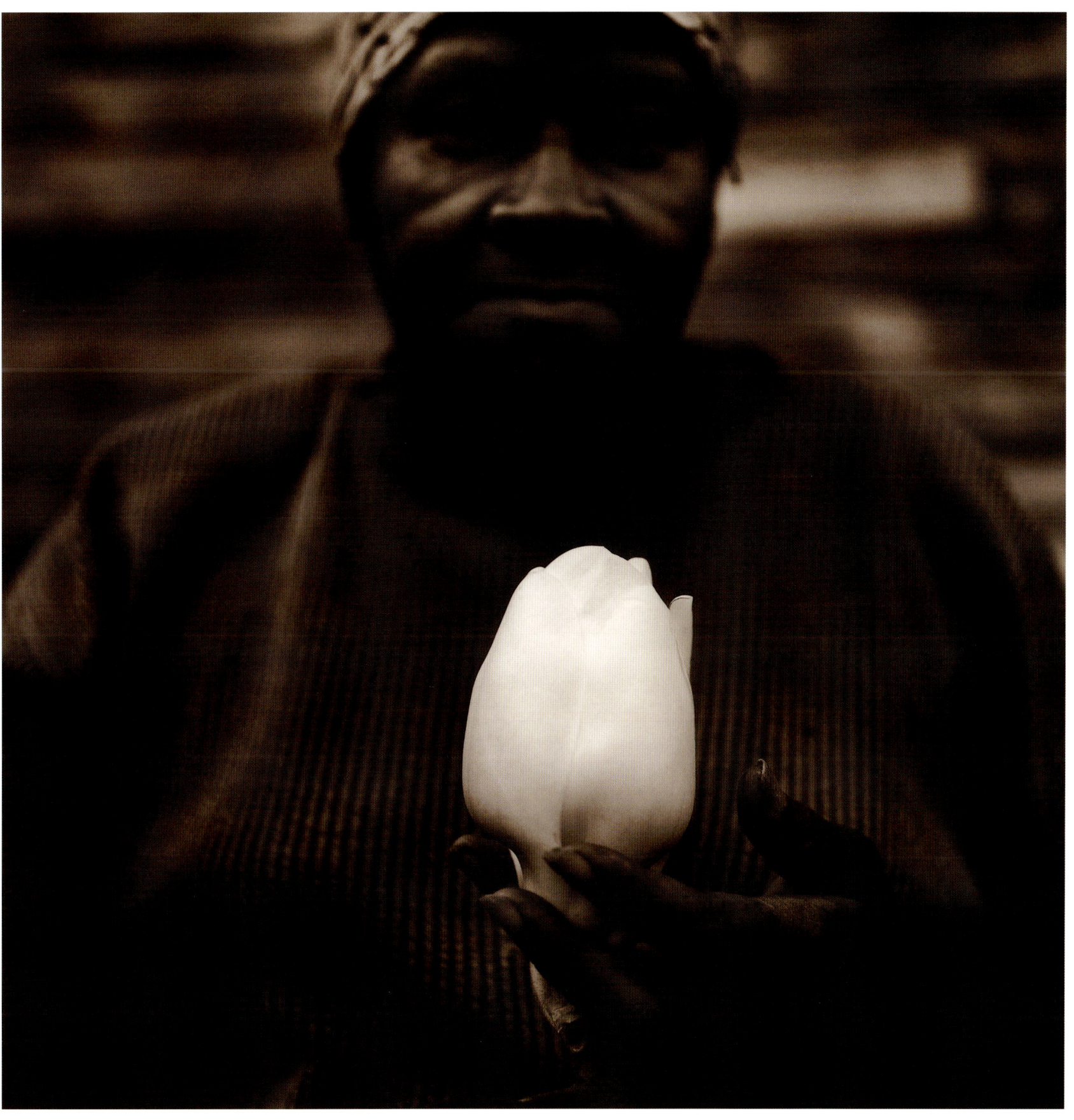

Brothers. 1996, Como, Miss.

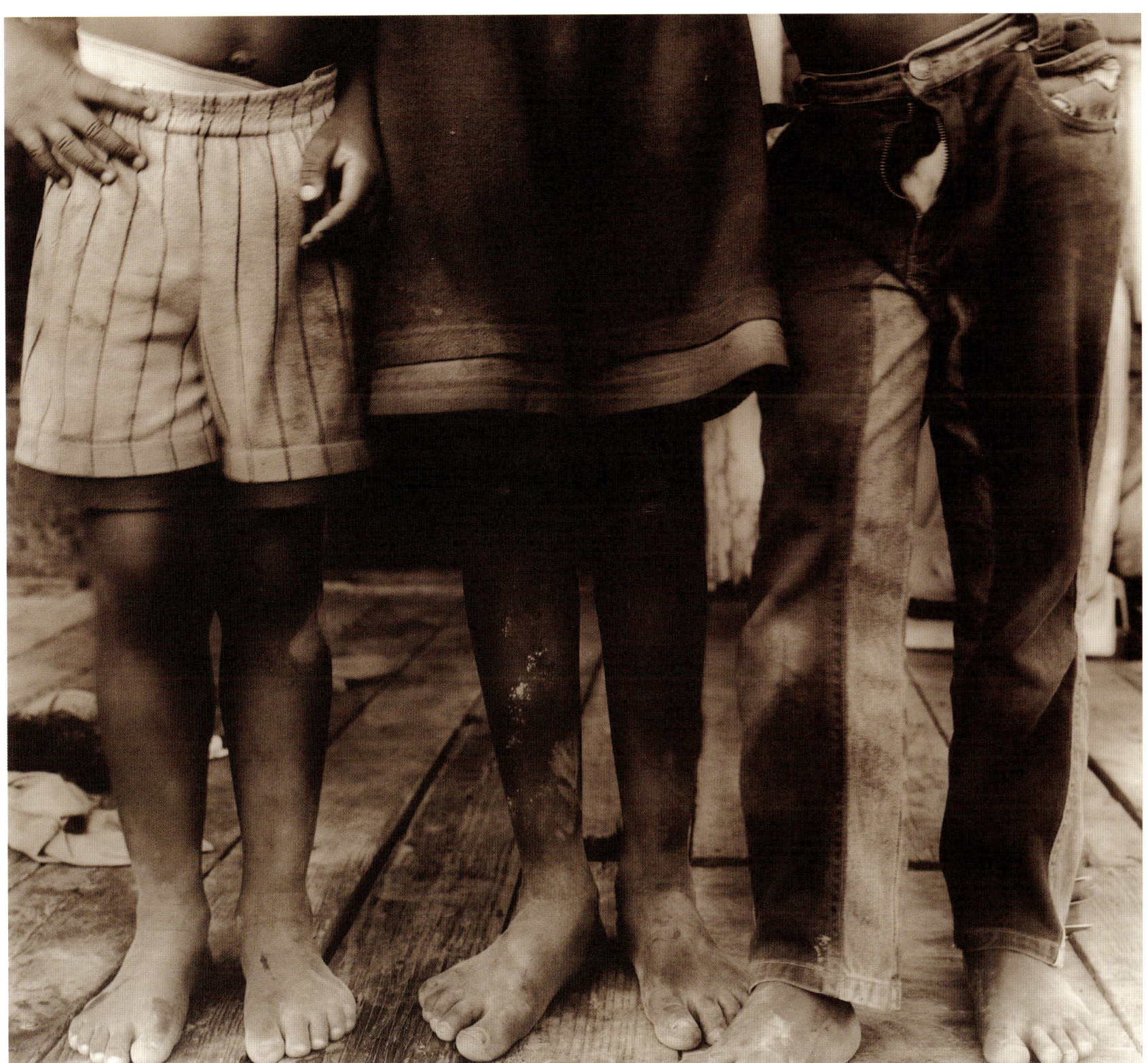

Girl with Sunflowers. 1996, Como, Miss.

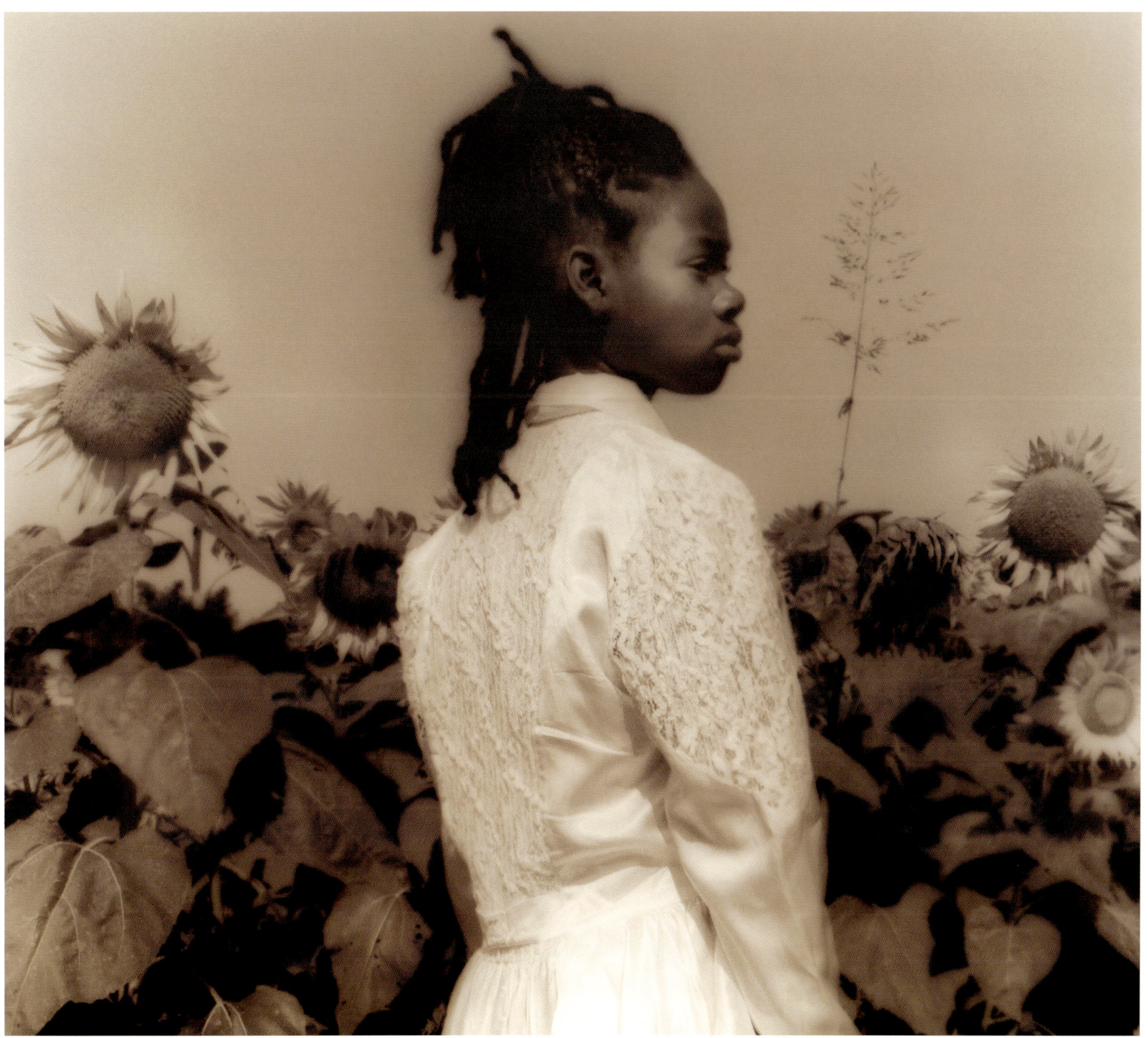

Sunday Dress. 1997, Moscow, Tenn.

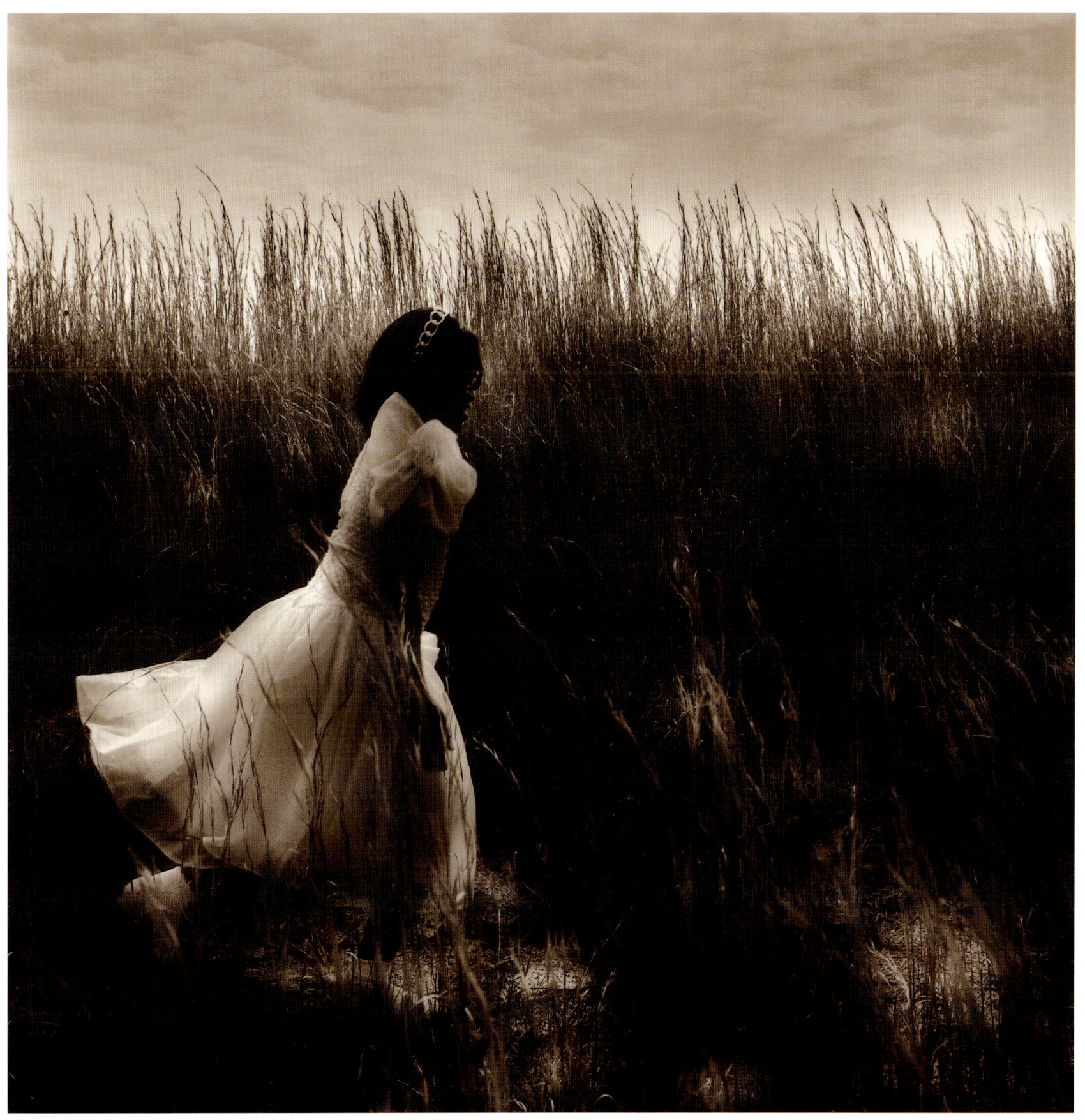

Boy with Ball. 1996, Como, Miss.

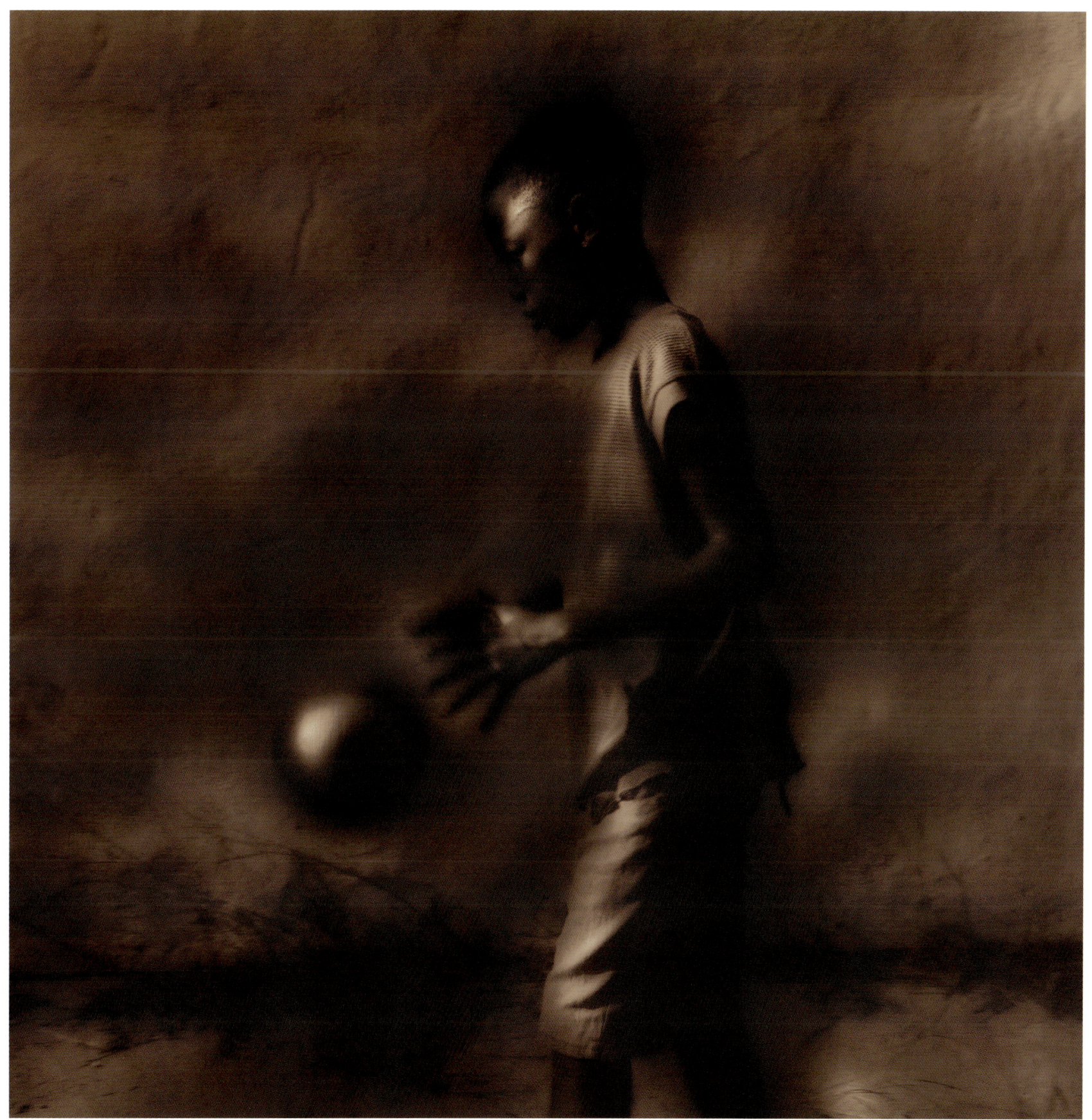

Happy Child. 1996, Como, Miss.

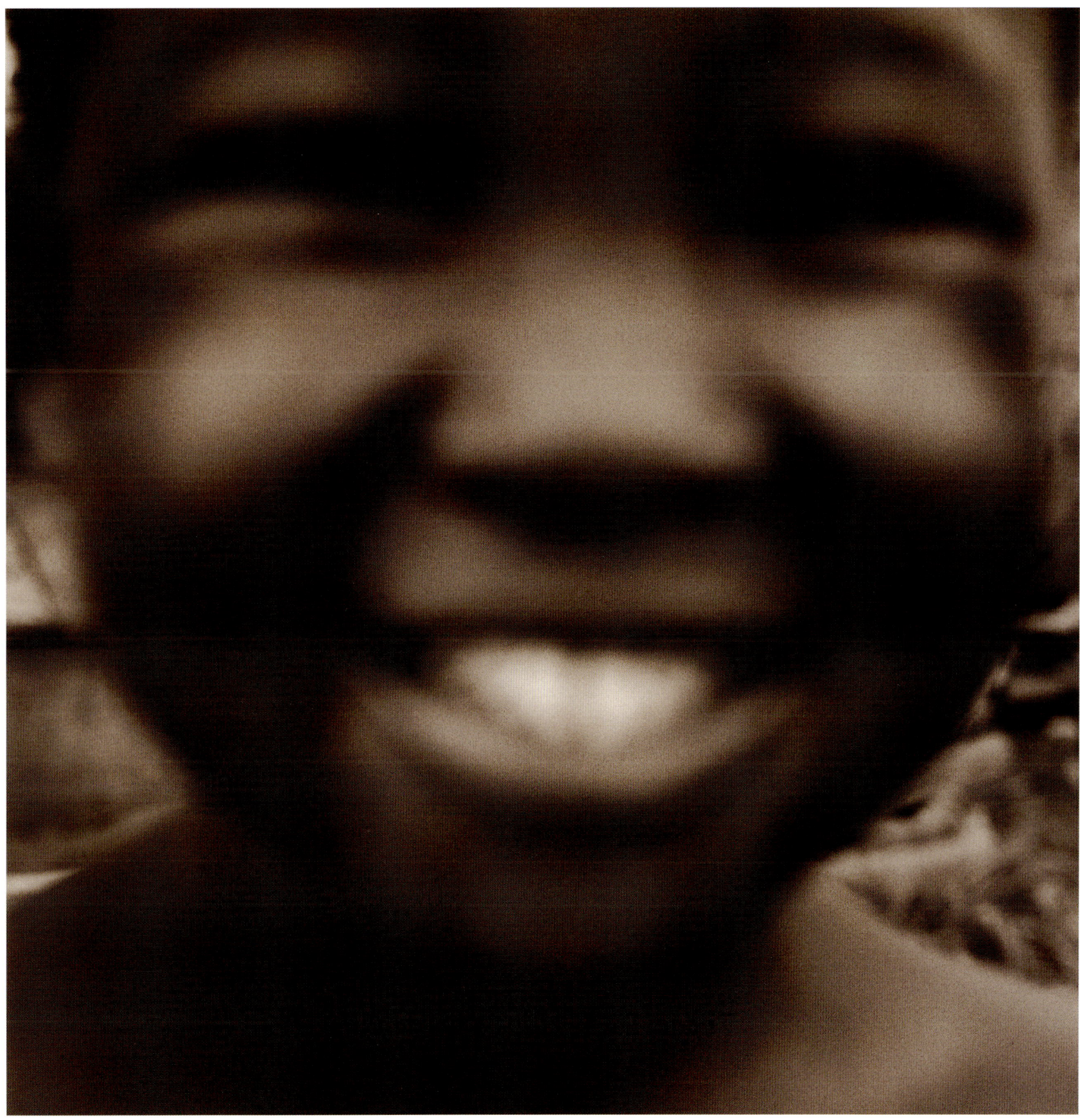

Girl on a Carousel. 1996, New Orleans.

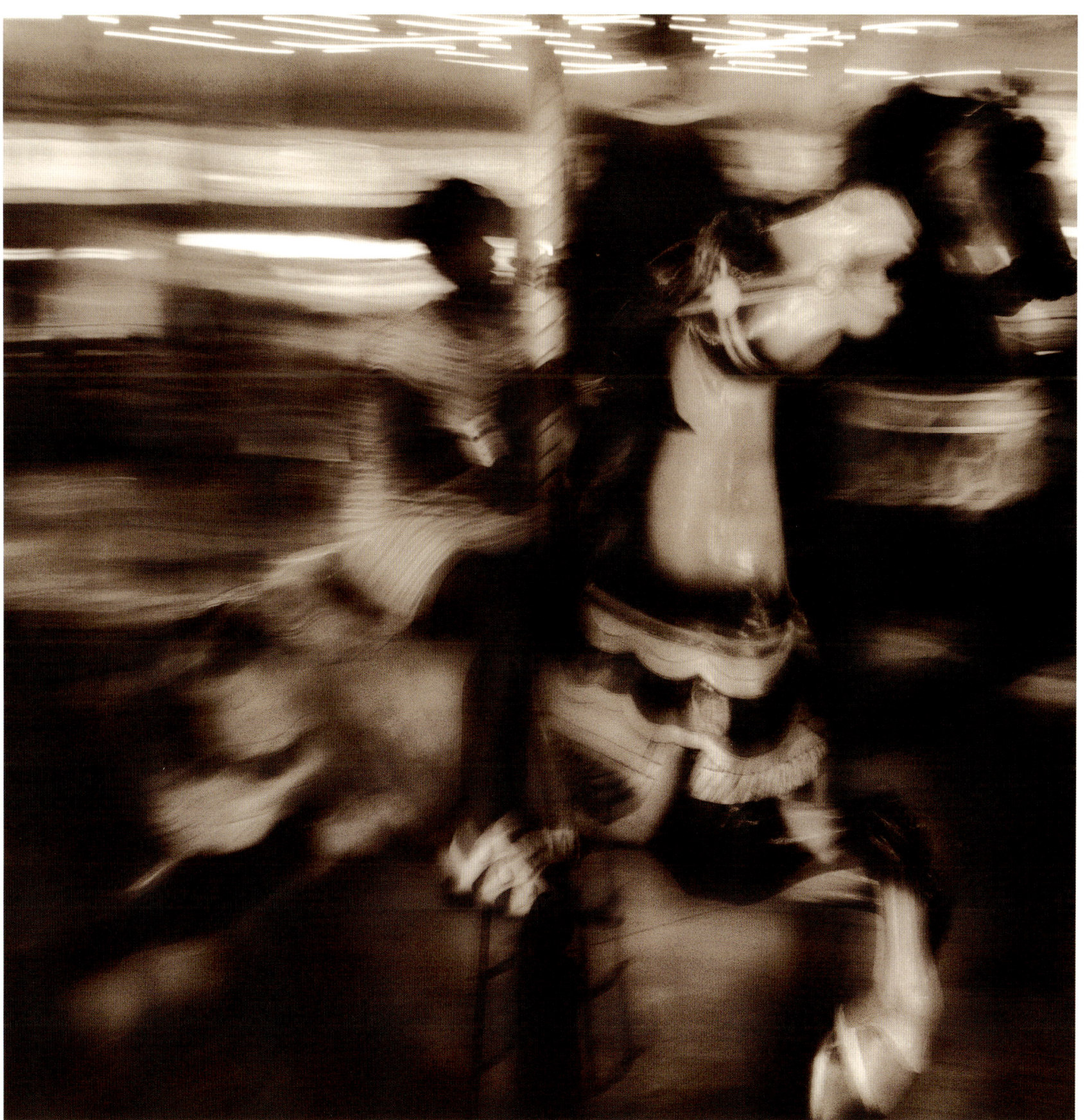

BICYCLERS. 1994, Greenville, Miss.

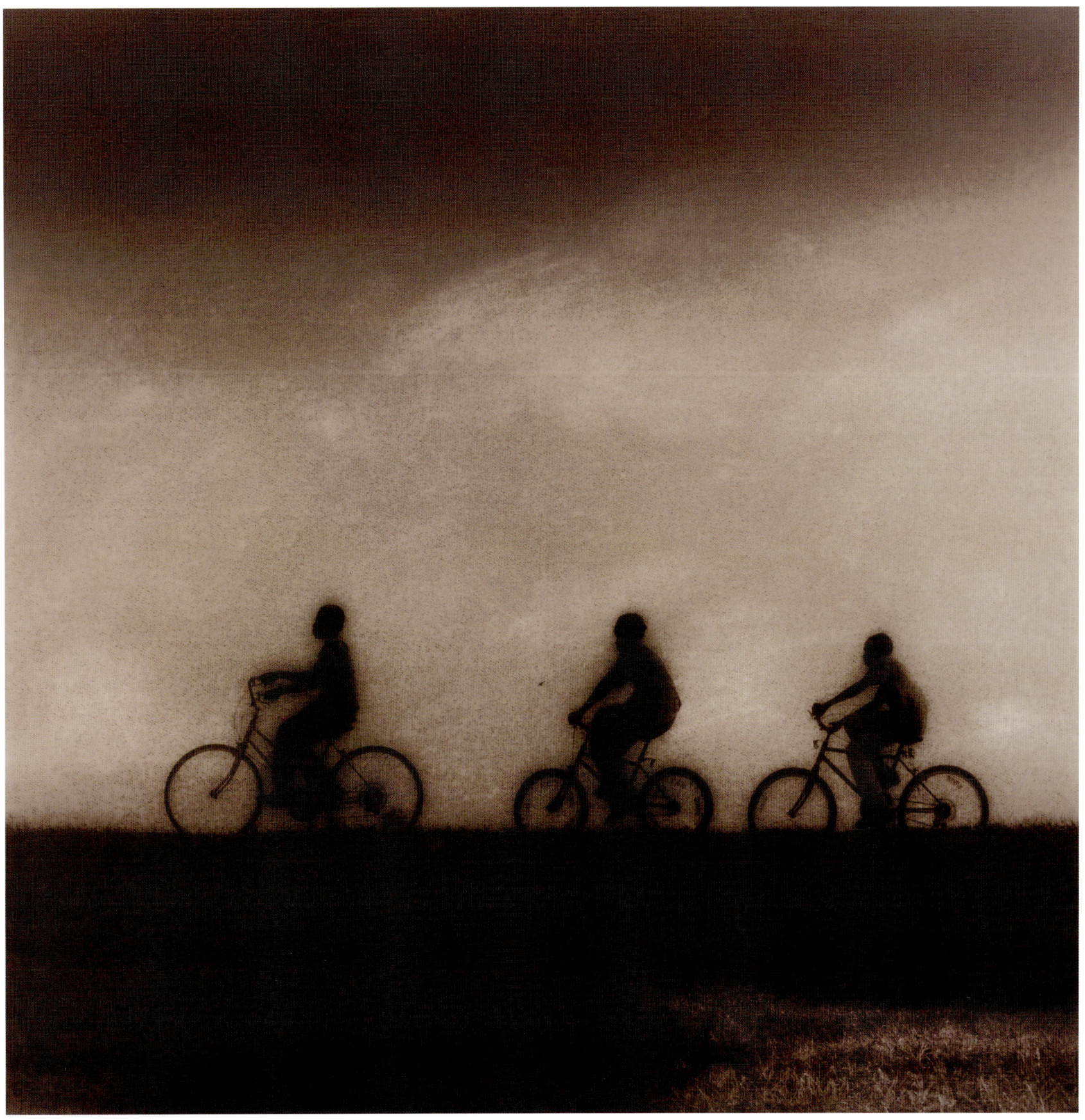

Tireswings. 1997, St. Landry Parish, La.

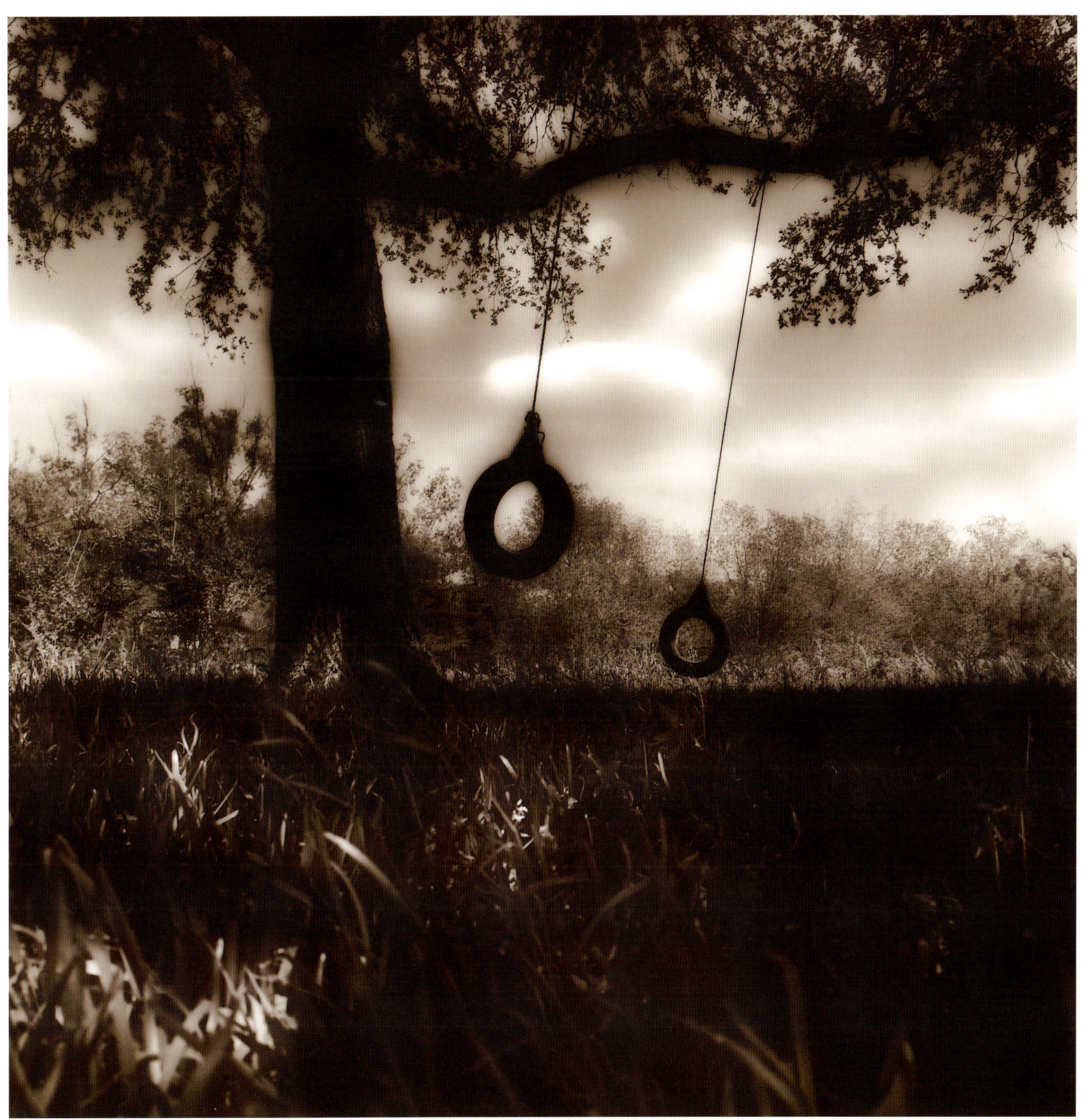

Junebug with Tire. 1995, Como, Miss.

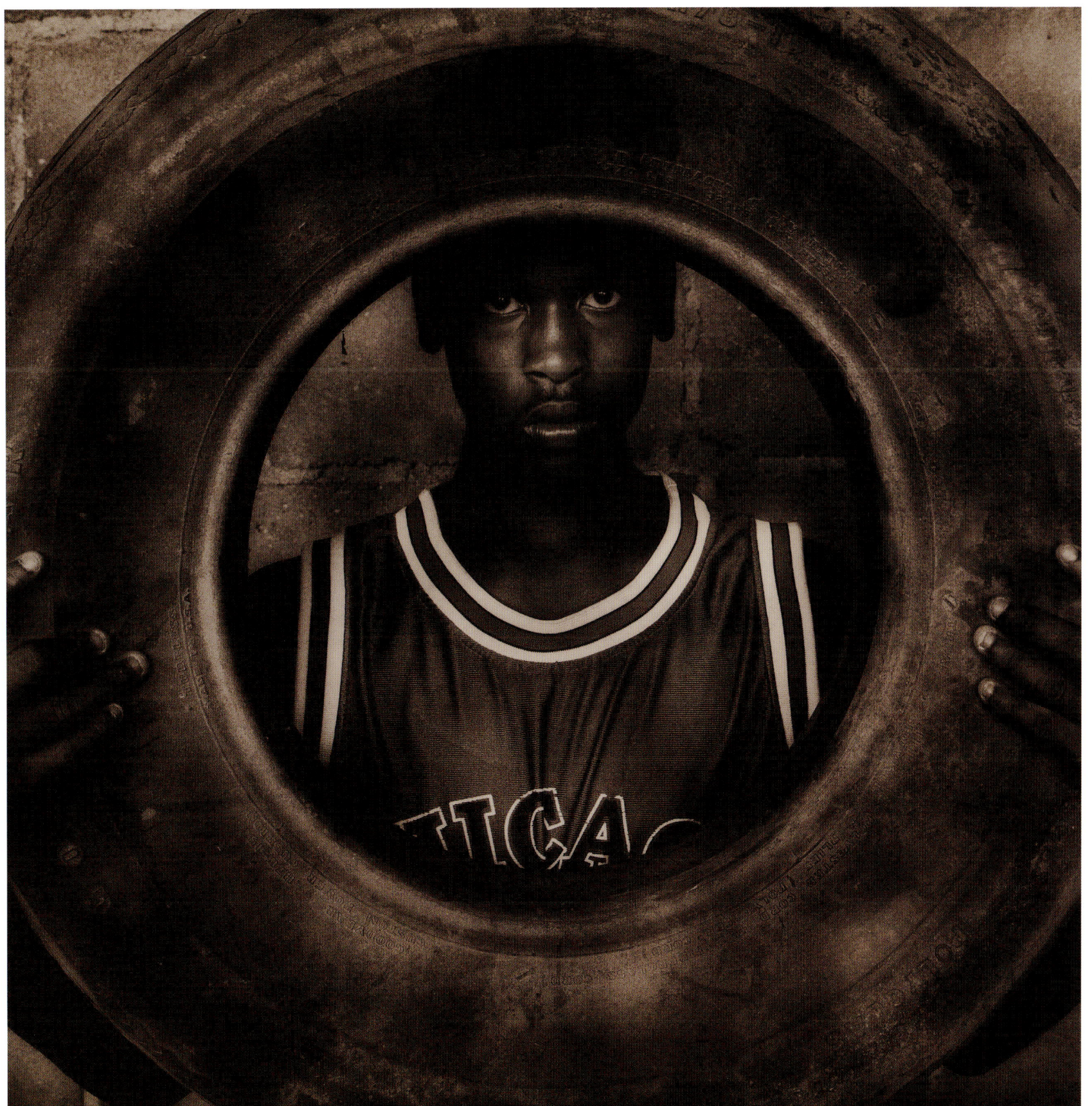

Corrugated Shadow. 1995, Como, Miss.

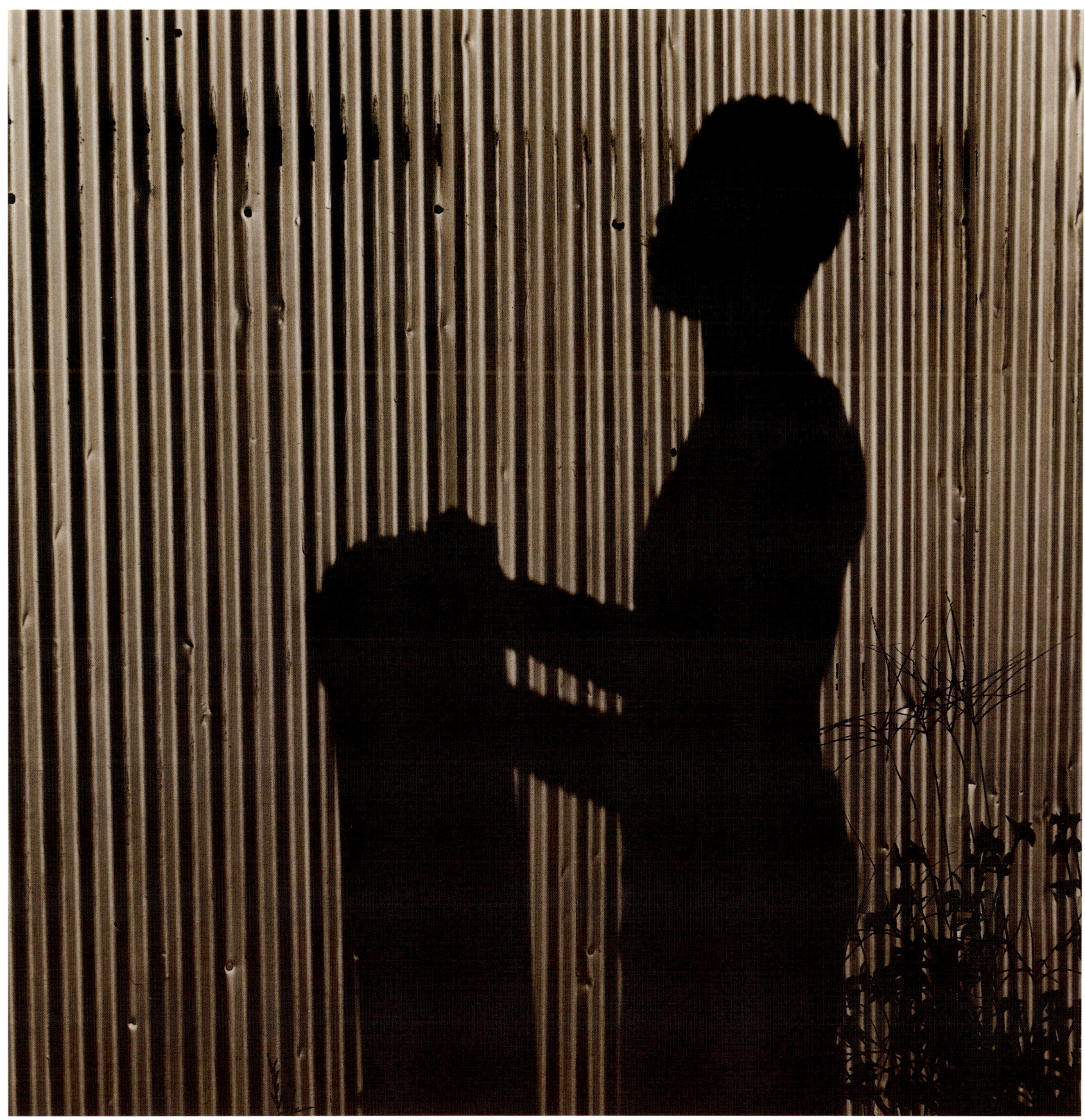

Man with Fish. 1995, Como, Miss.

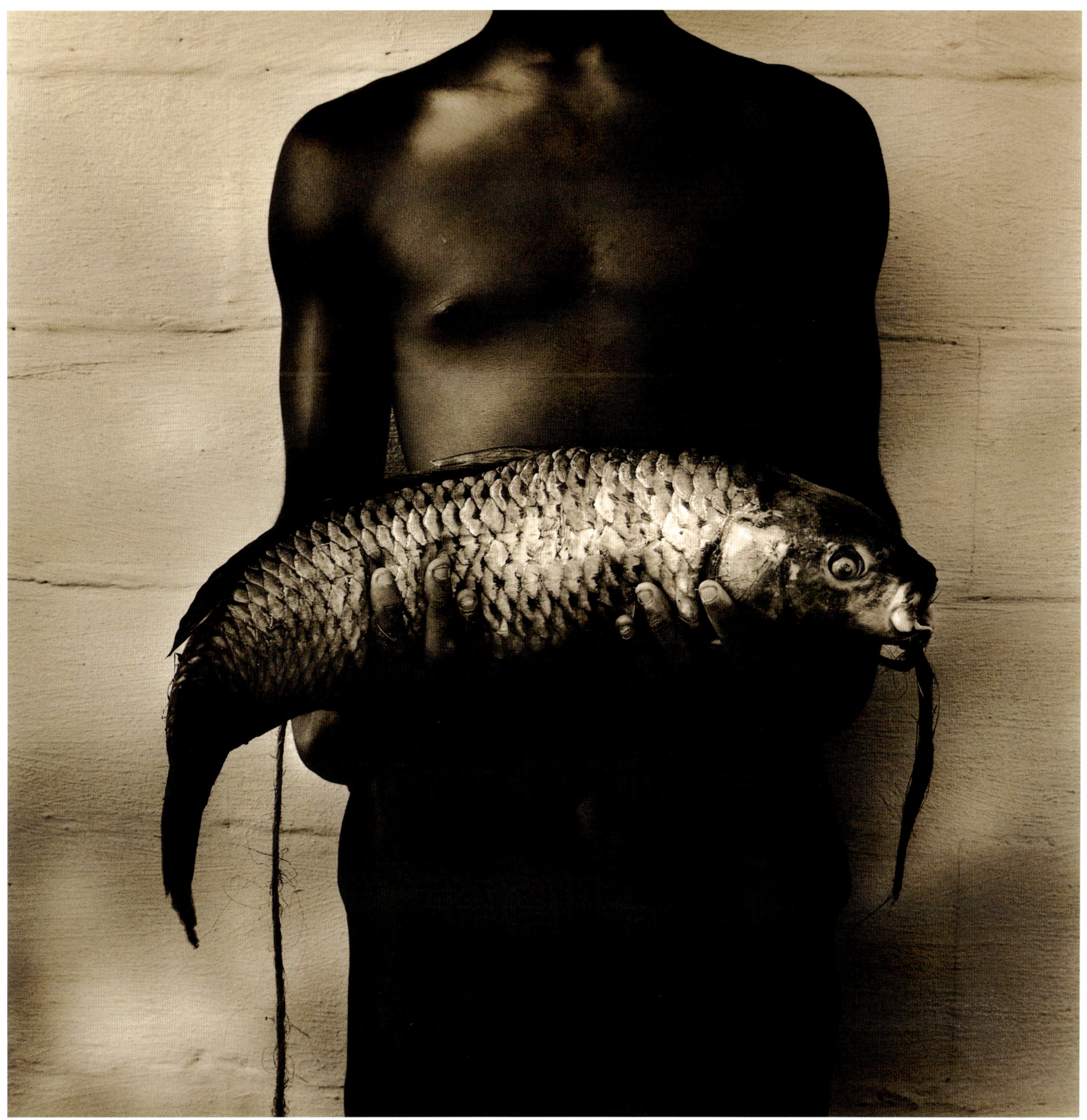

Tomotley. 1998, South Carolina.

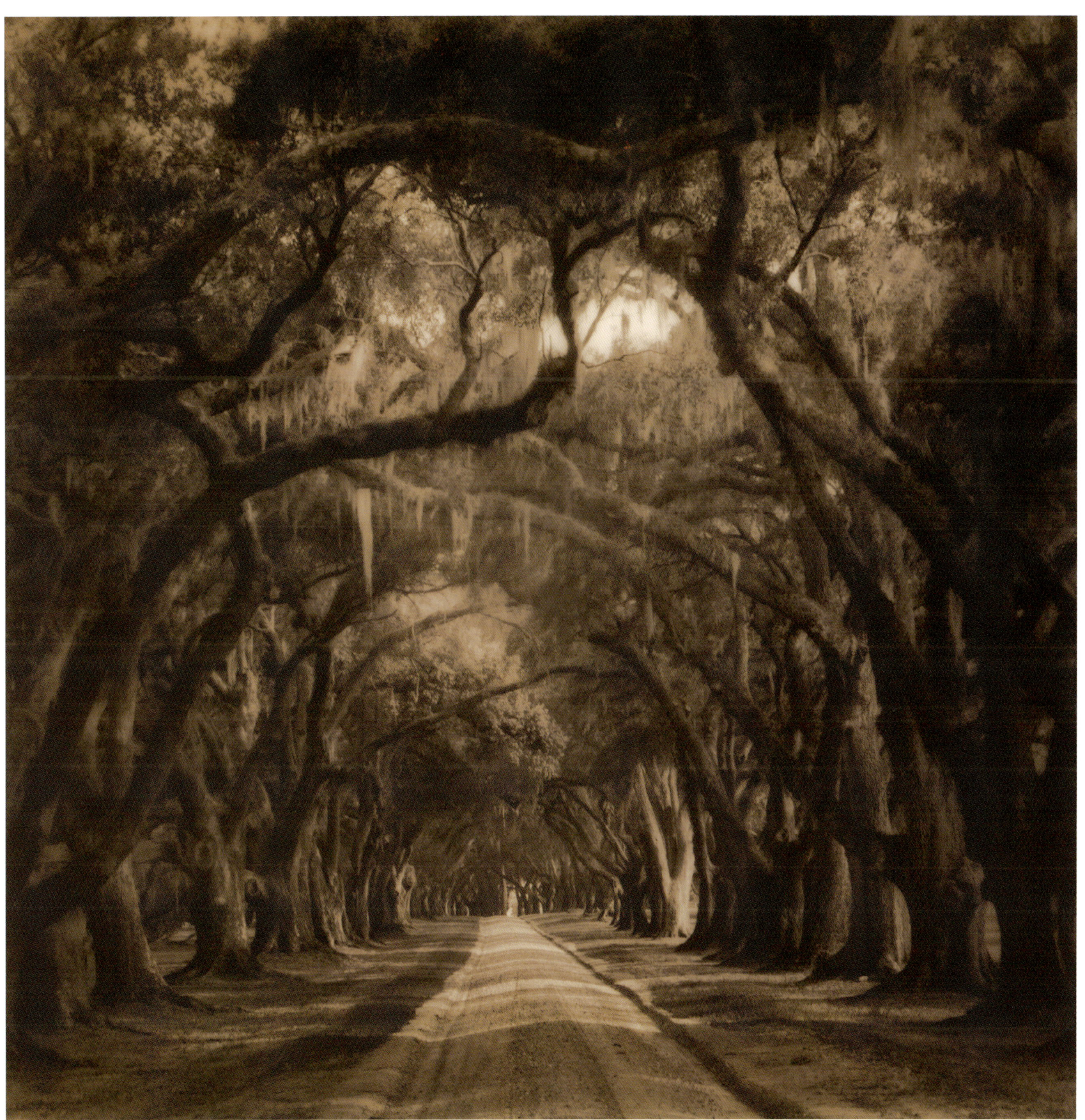

Sheldon Church Ruins (burned by General Sherman in 1865). 1998, Sheldon, S.C.

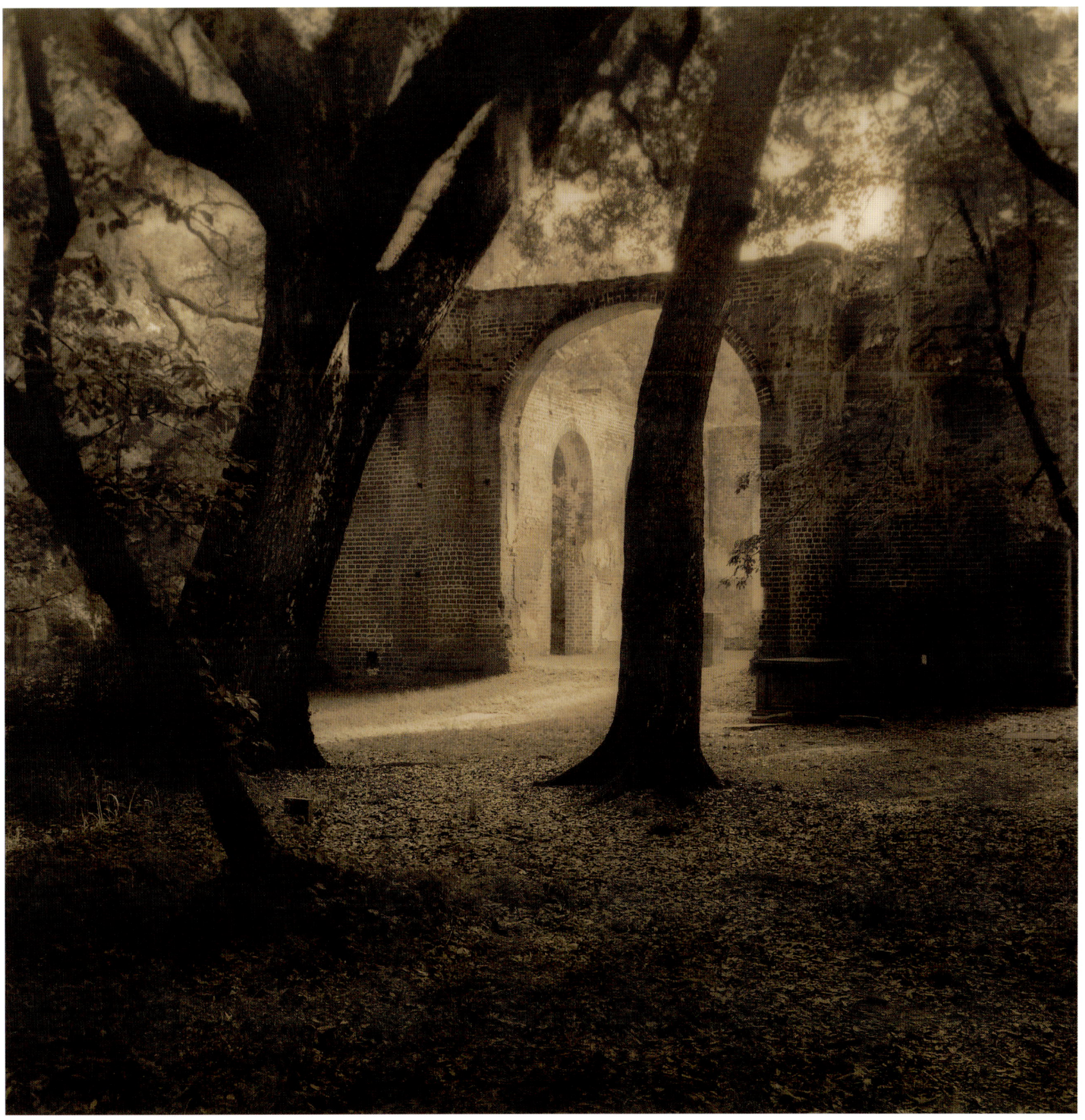

Reverend Dennis in Prayer. 1997, Vicksburg, Miss.

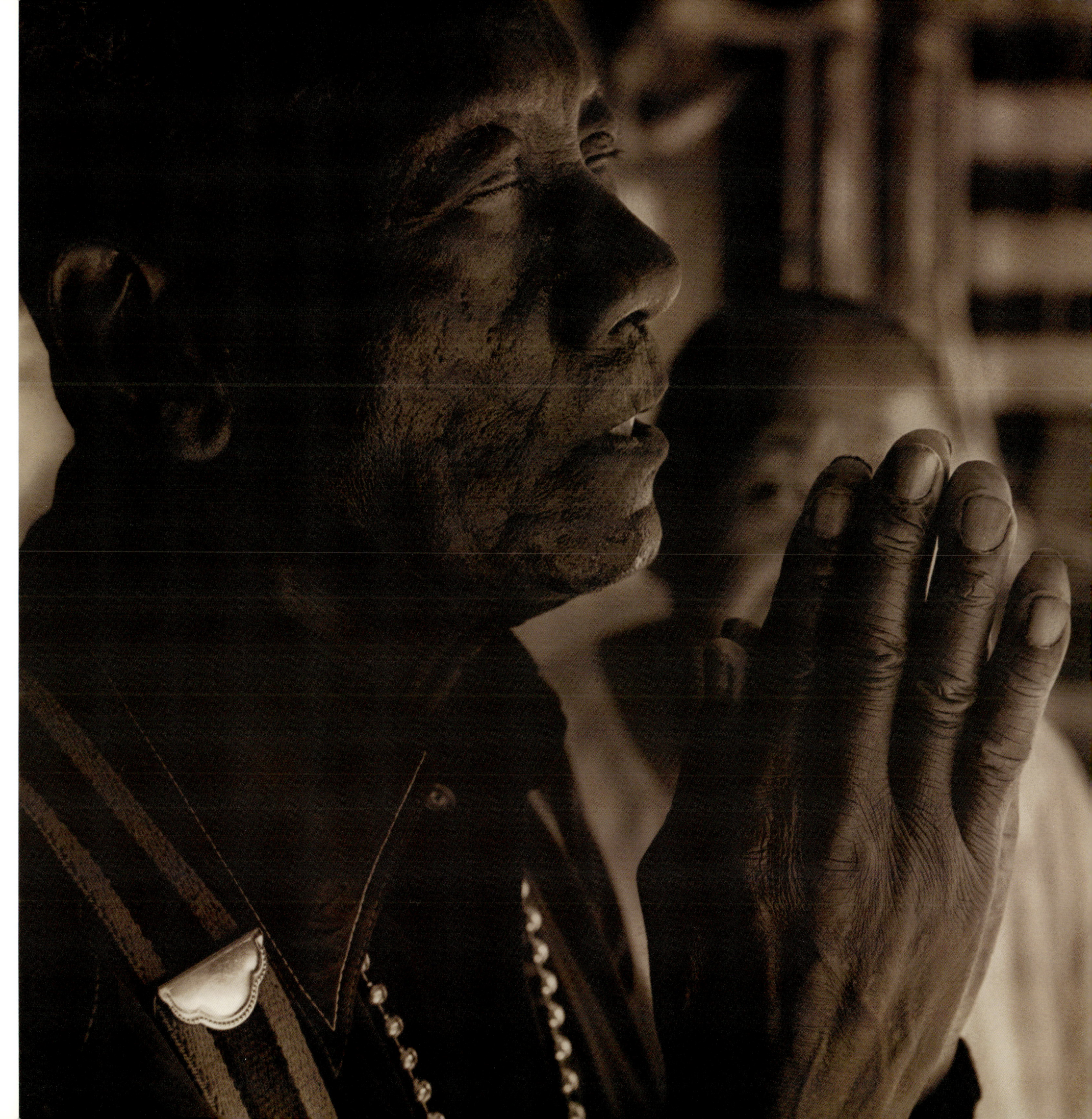

Reverend Dennis. 1997, Vicksburg, Miss.

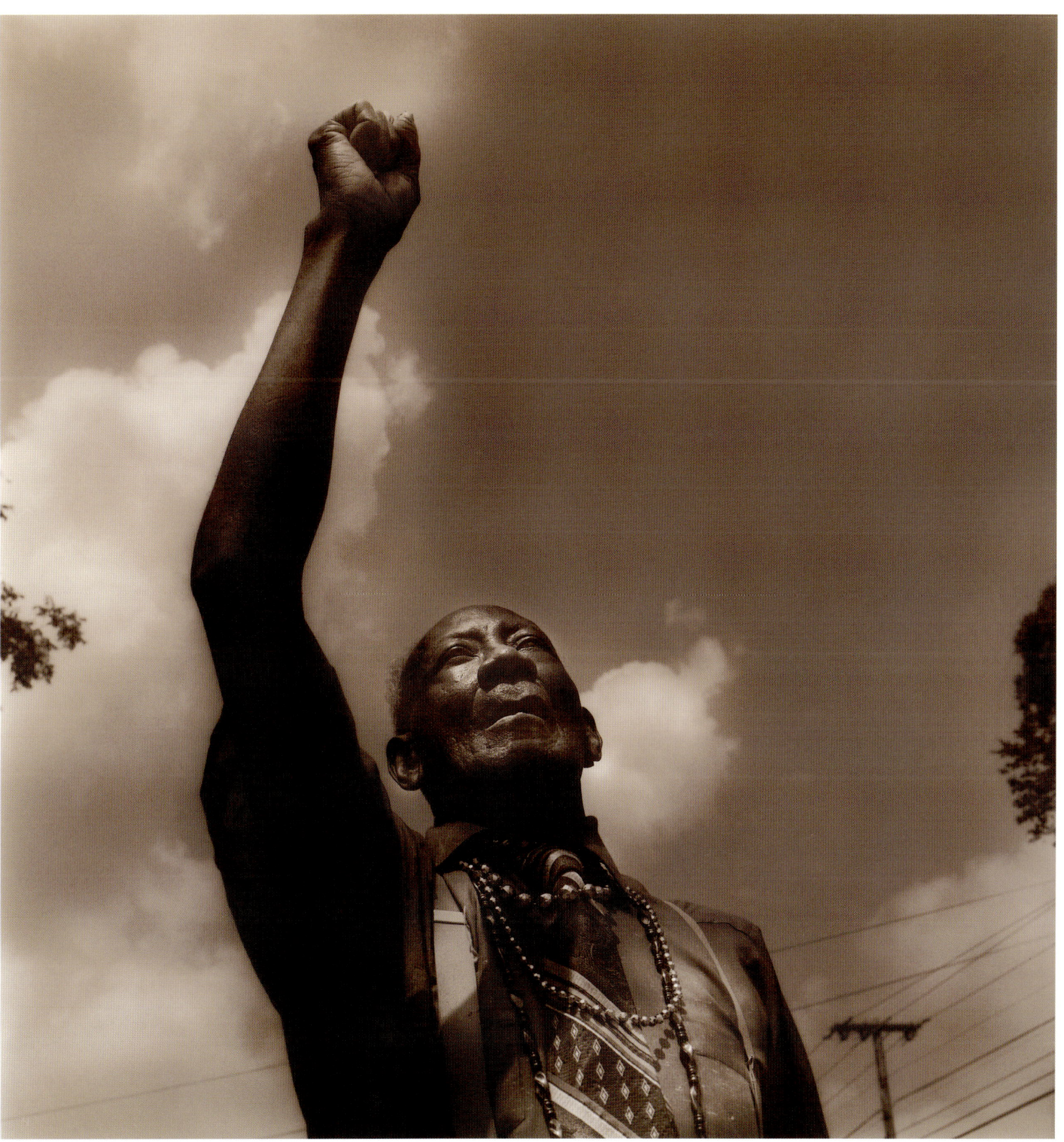

Reverend Stokes's Baptismal Pool. 1996, Marks, Miss.

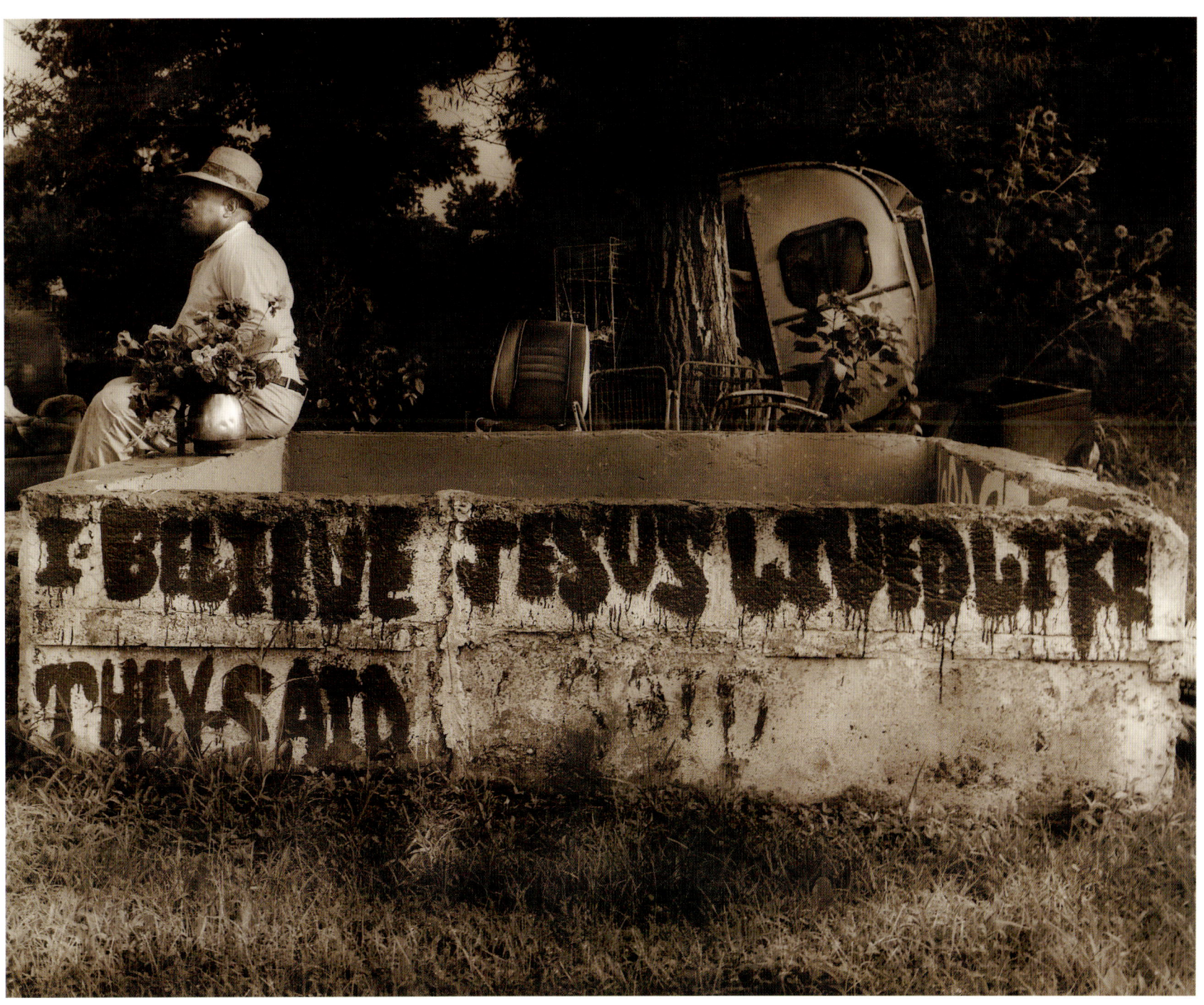

Songs of Faith. 1995, Como, Miss.

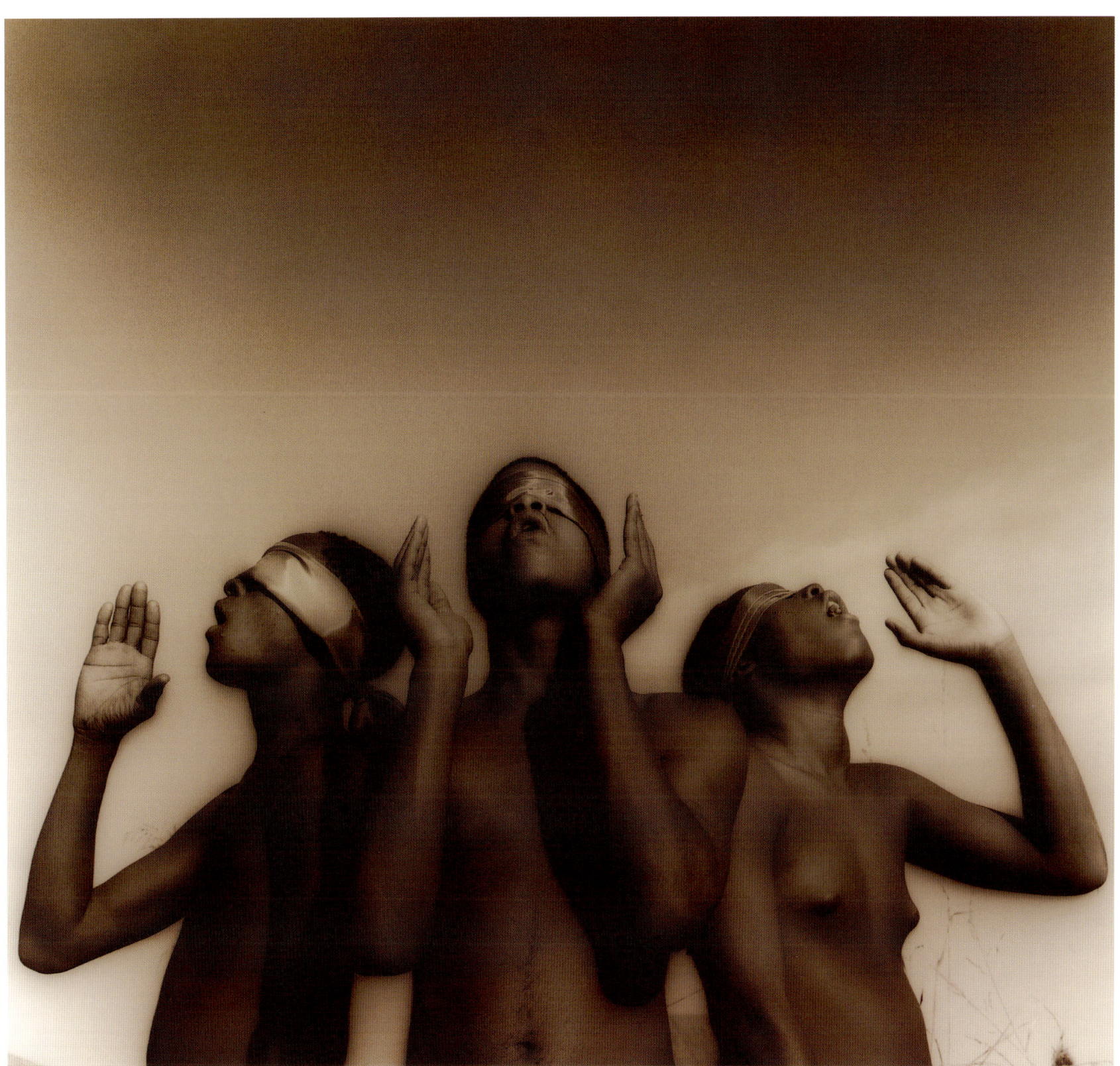

Baptismal Candidates. 1995, Moon Lake, Miss.

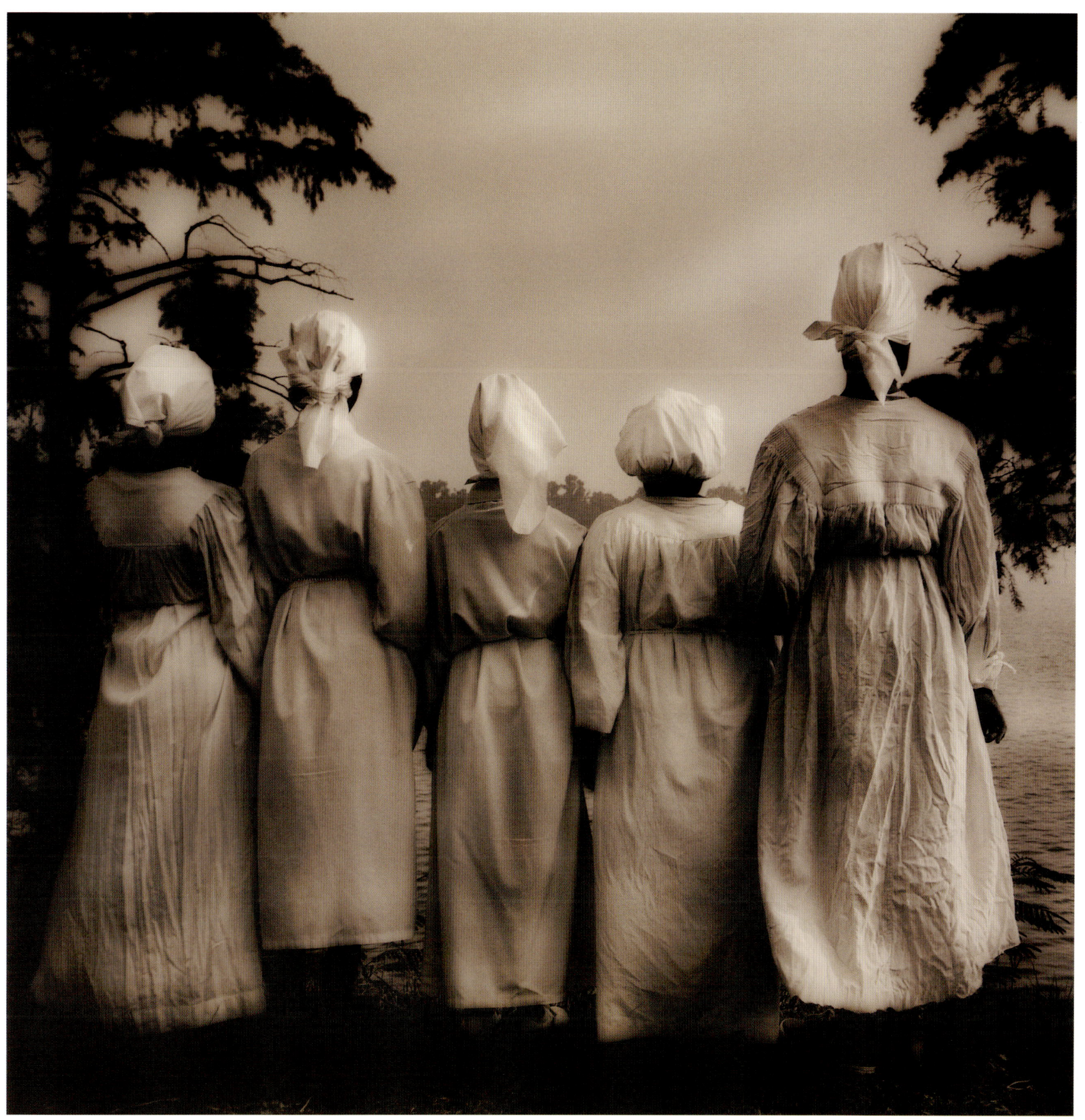

Resurrection Flags. 1995, Como, Miss.

Overleaf:
Trees and Smoke No. 1. 1998, Grand Coteau, La.
Trees and Smoke No. 2. 1998, Grand Coteau, La.

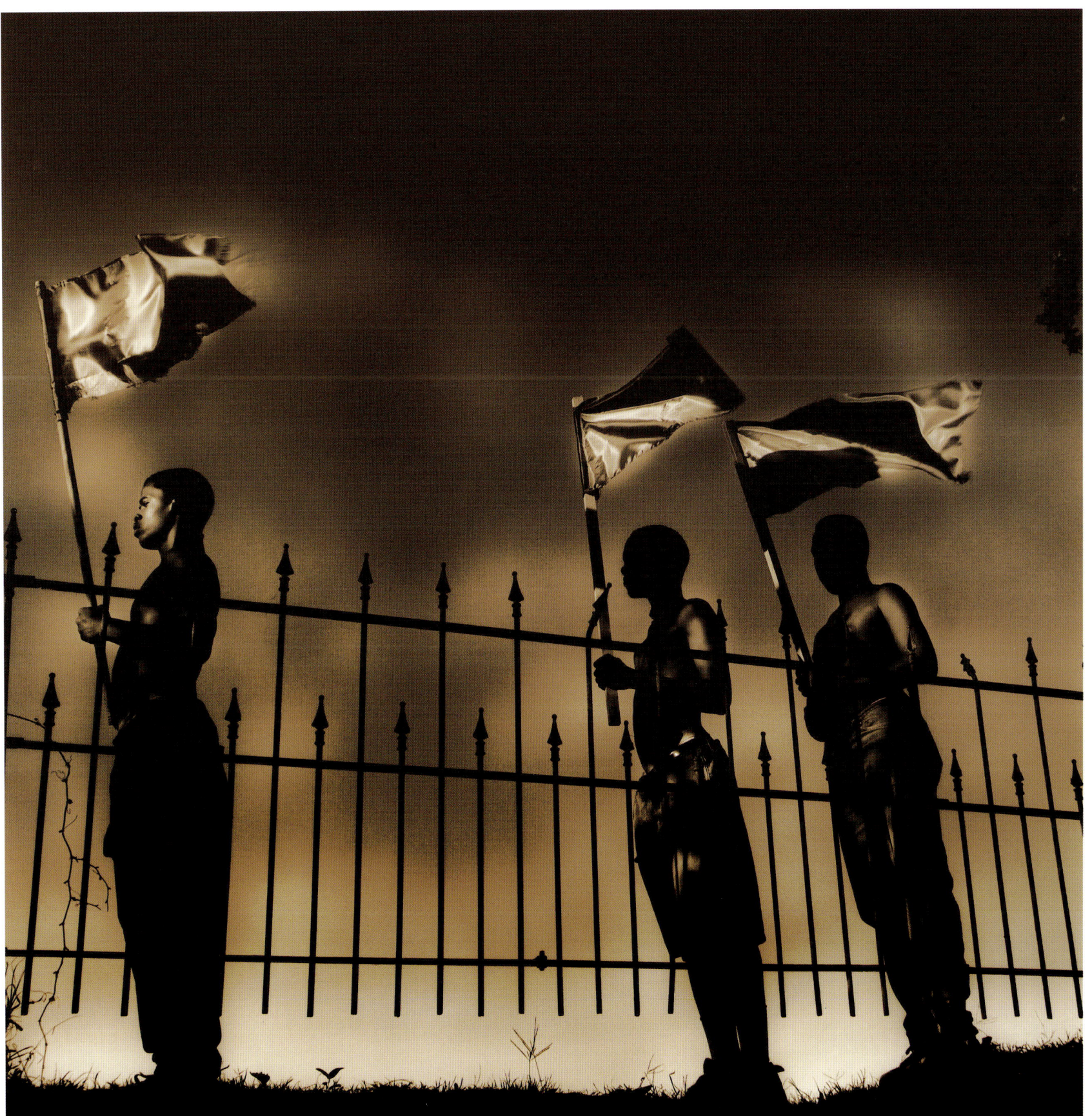

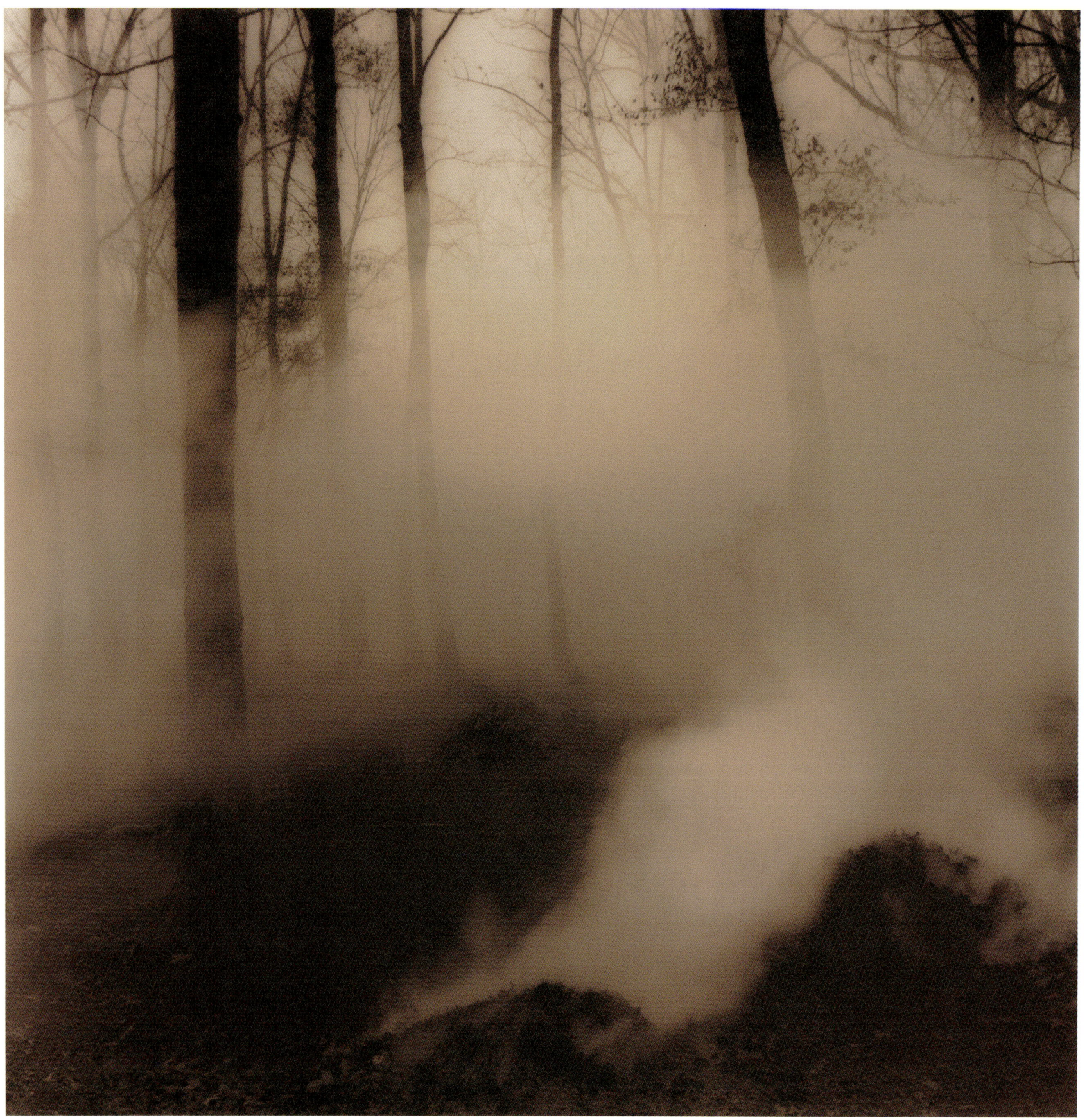

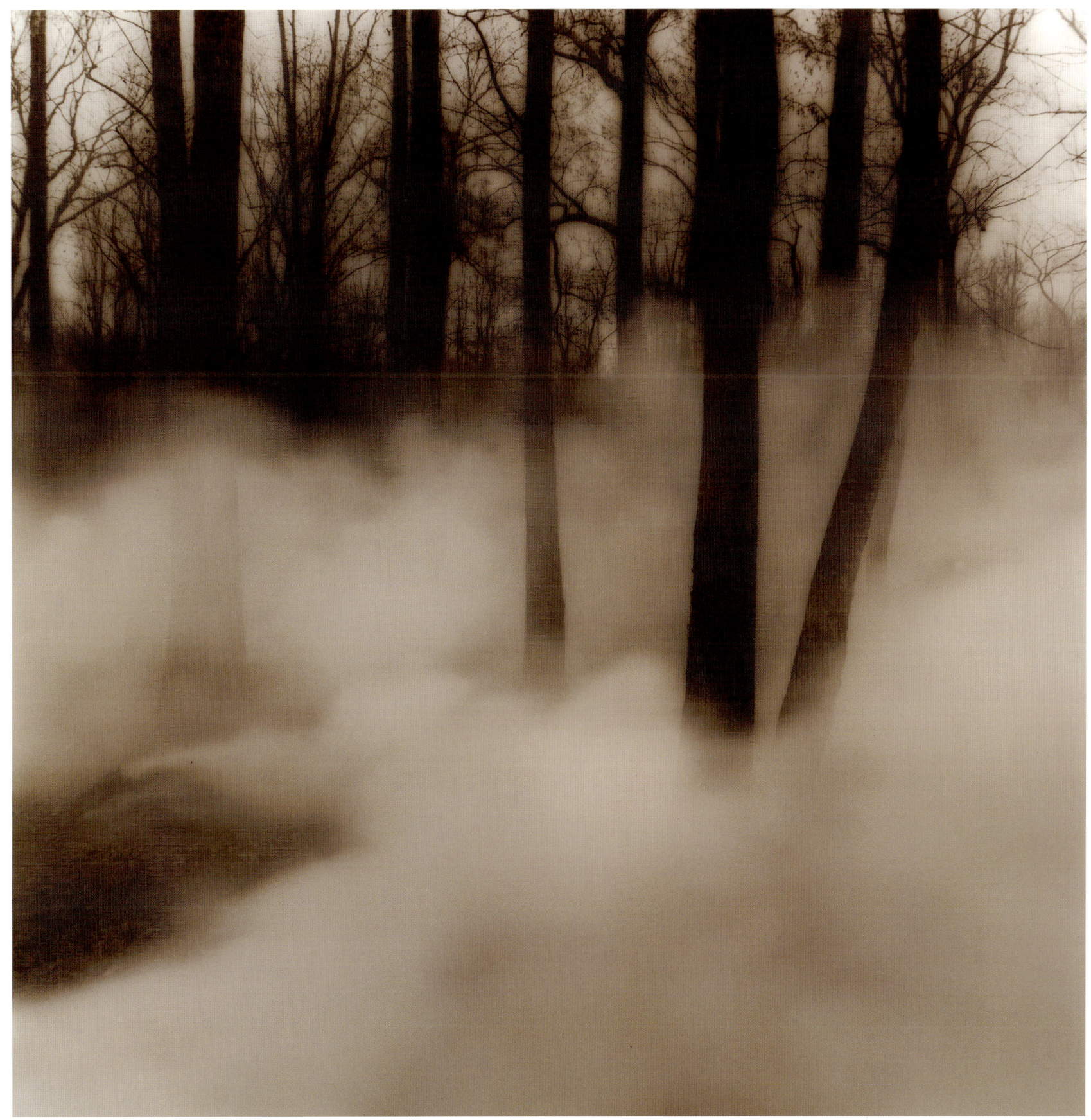

BLACKJACK ROAD. 1998, southern Virginia.

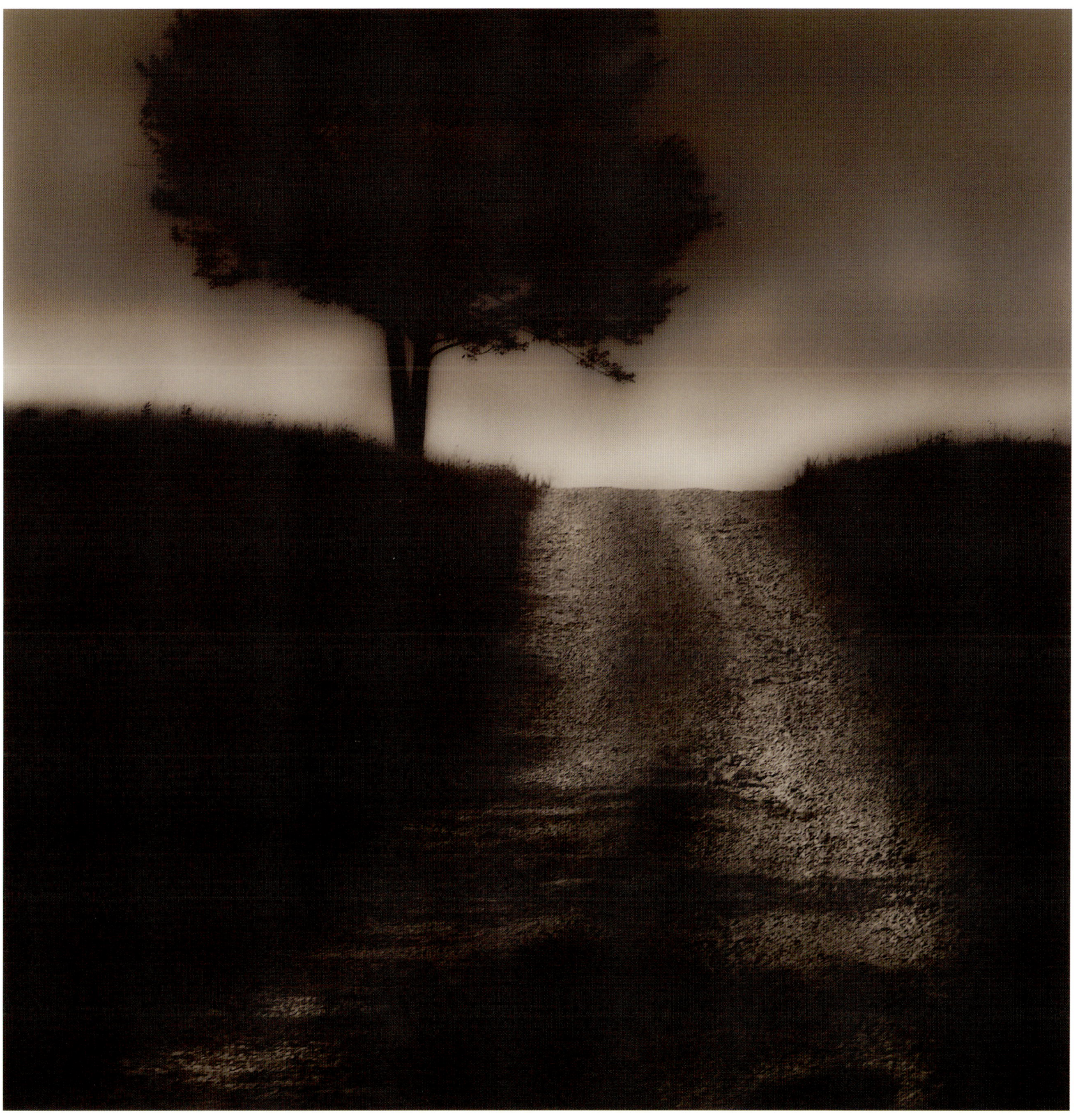

Juke Joint Window with Spray Paint and Grafitti. 1998, Vaiden, Miss.

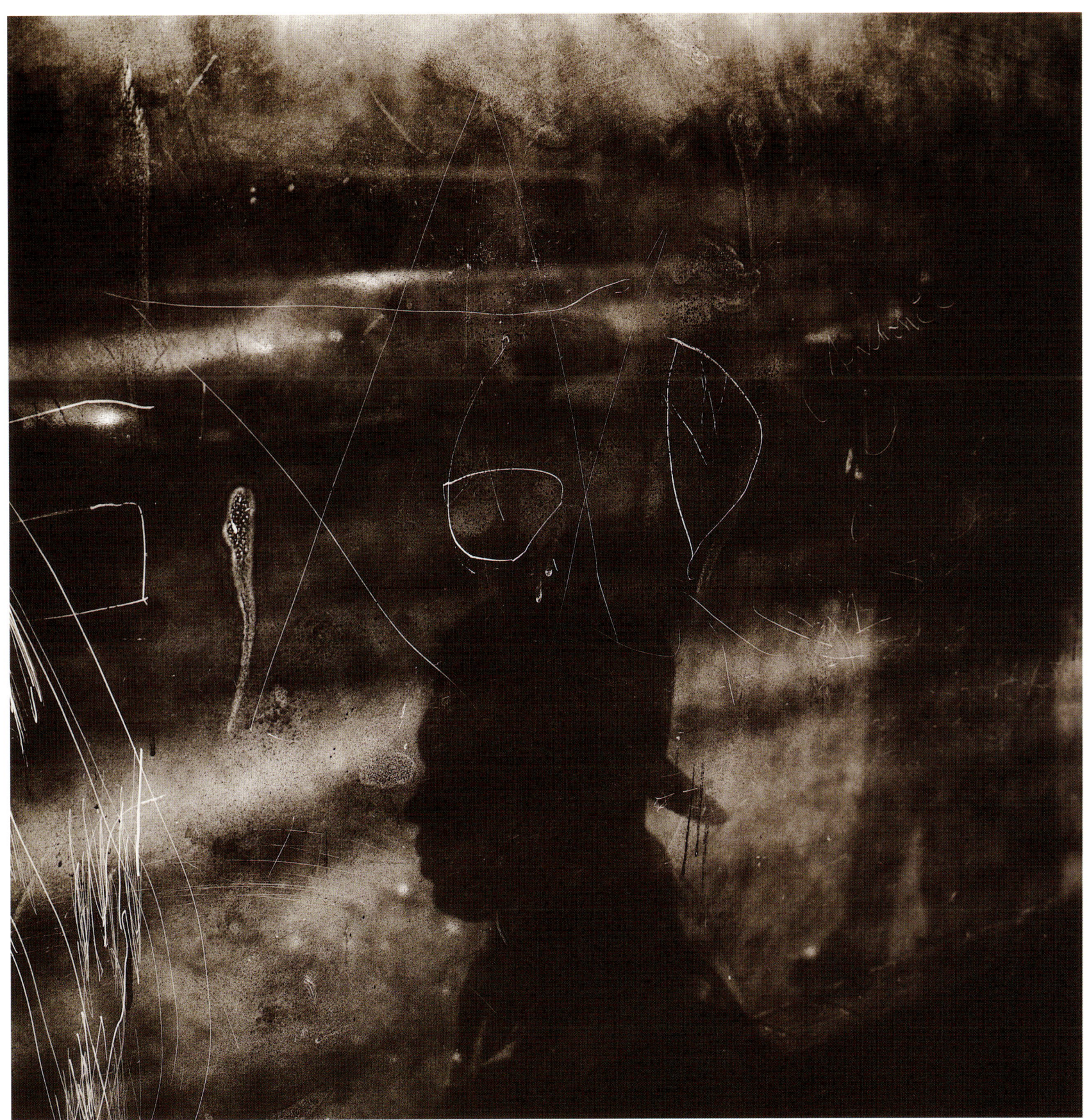

Amorous Window. 1996, Crenshaw, Miss.

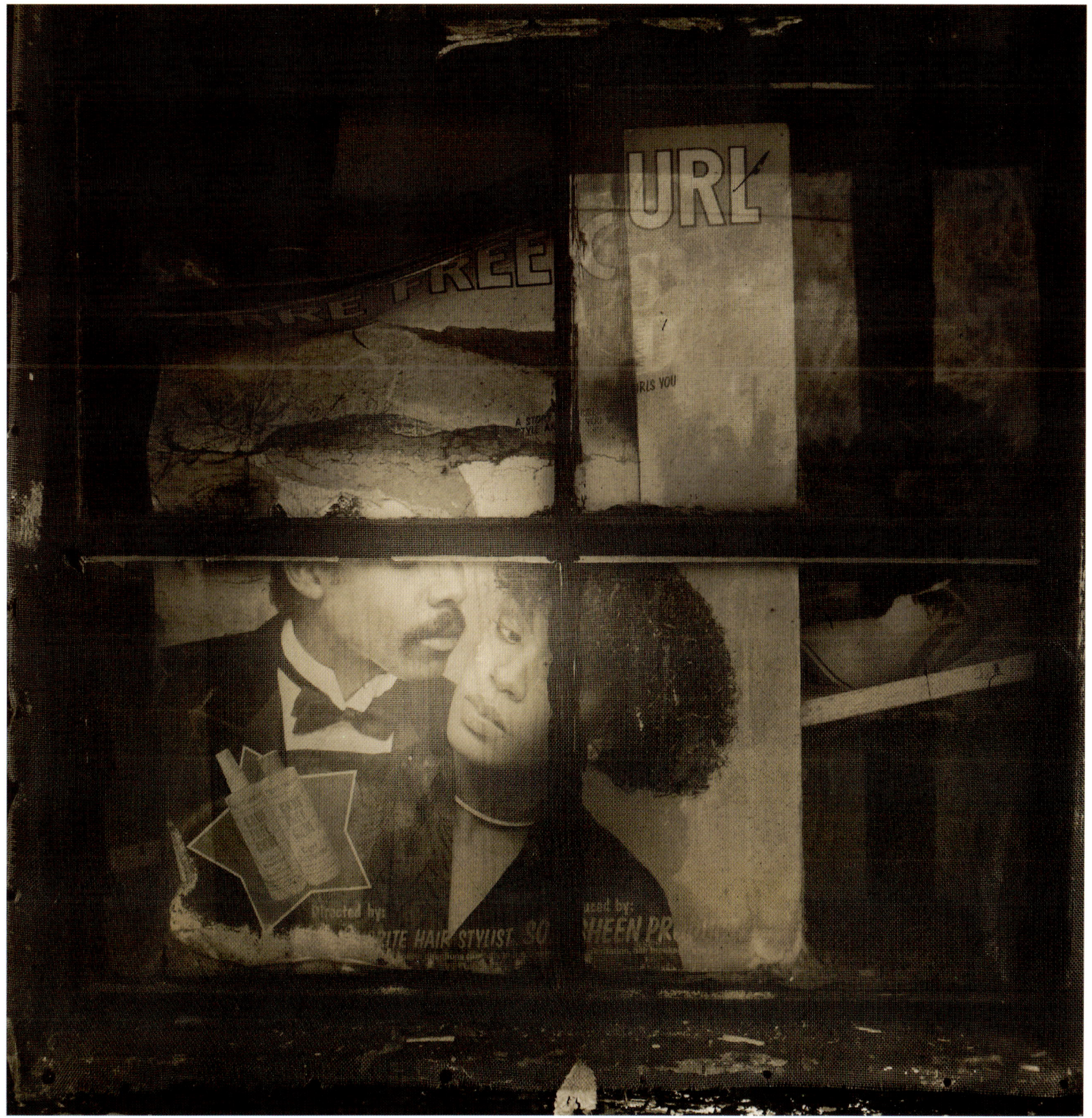

Isaac. 1998, Hollywood, S.C.

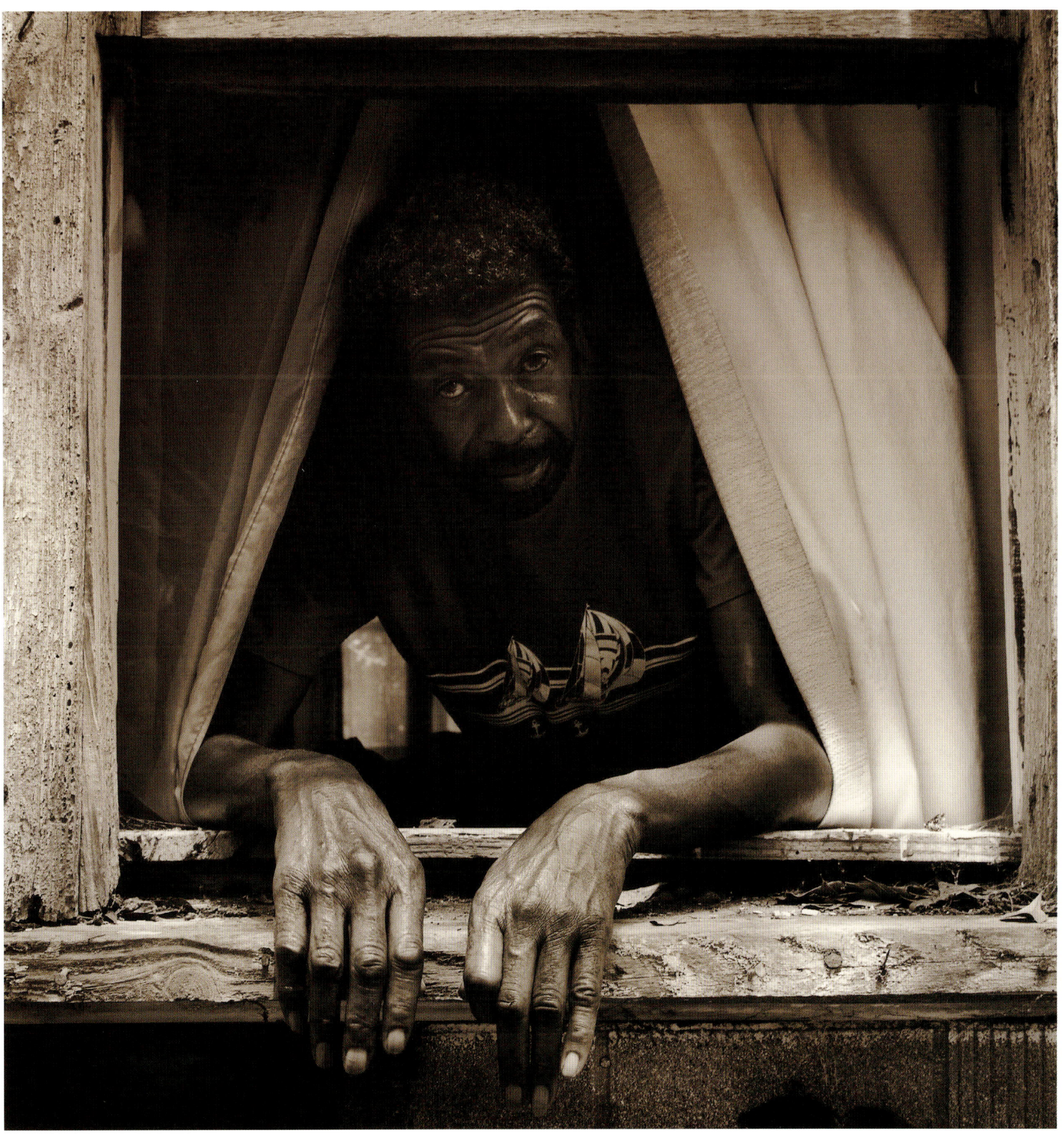

Jack Owens.   1996, Bentonia, Miss.

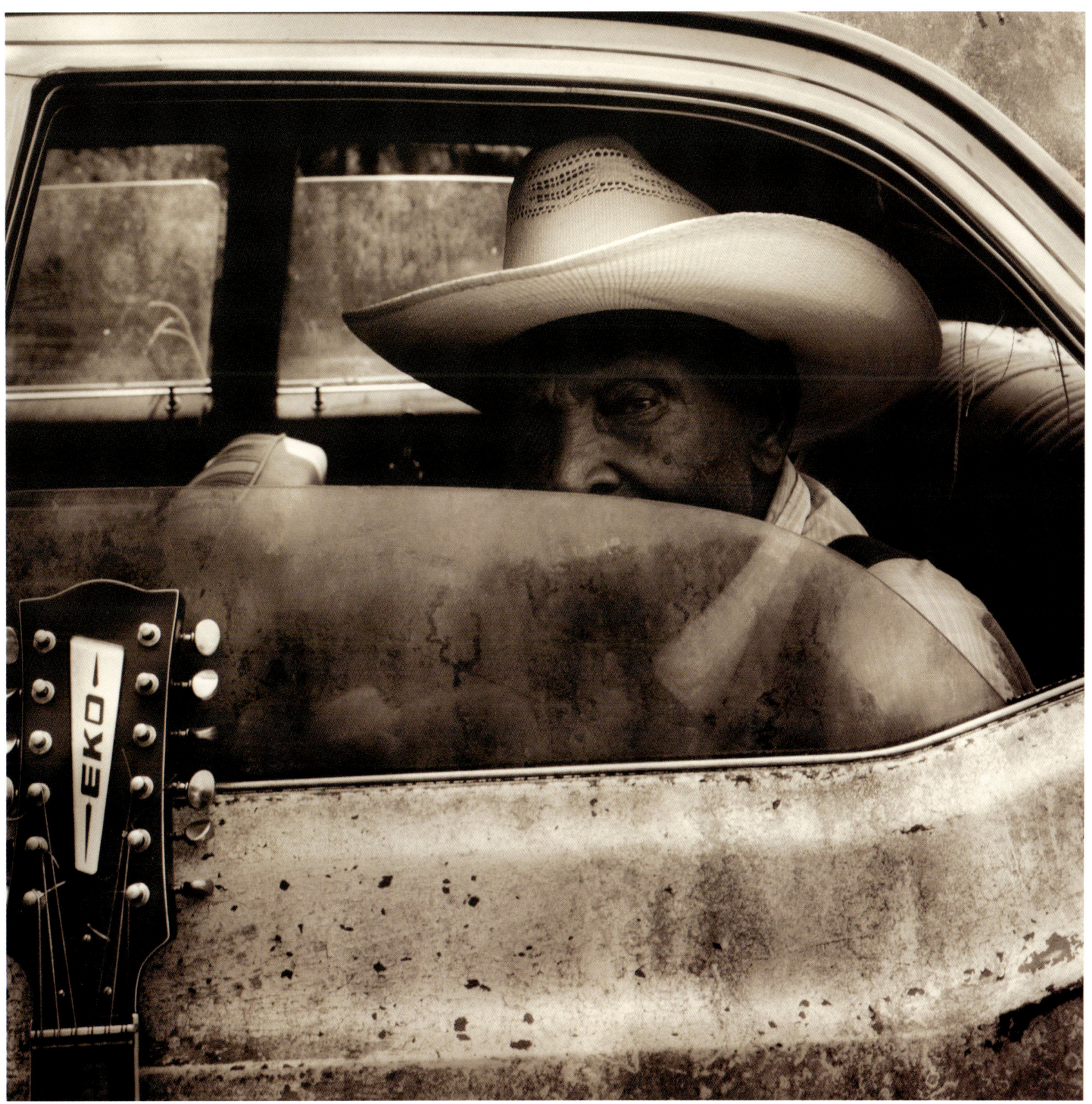

Three Seiners.   1995, Le Flore County, Miss.

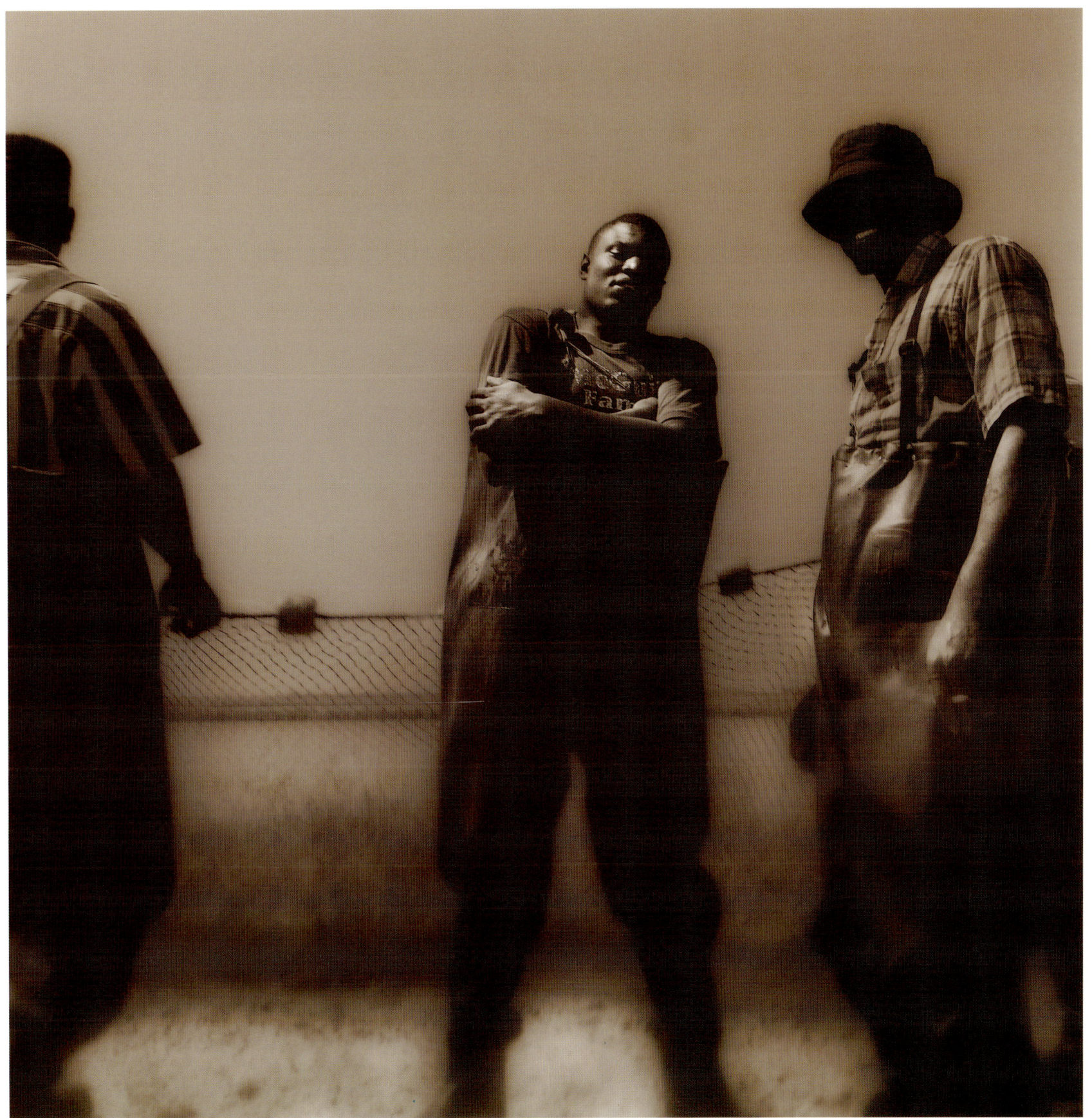

Razorblade. 1998, Clarksdale, Miss.

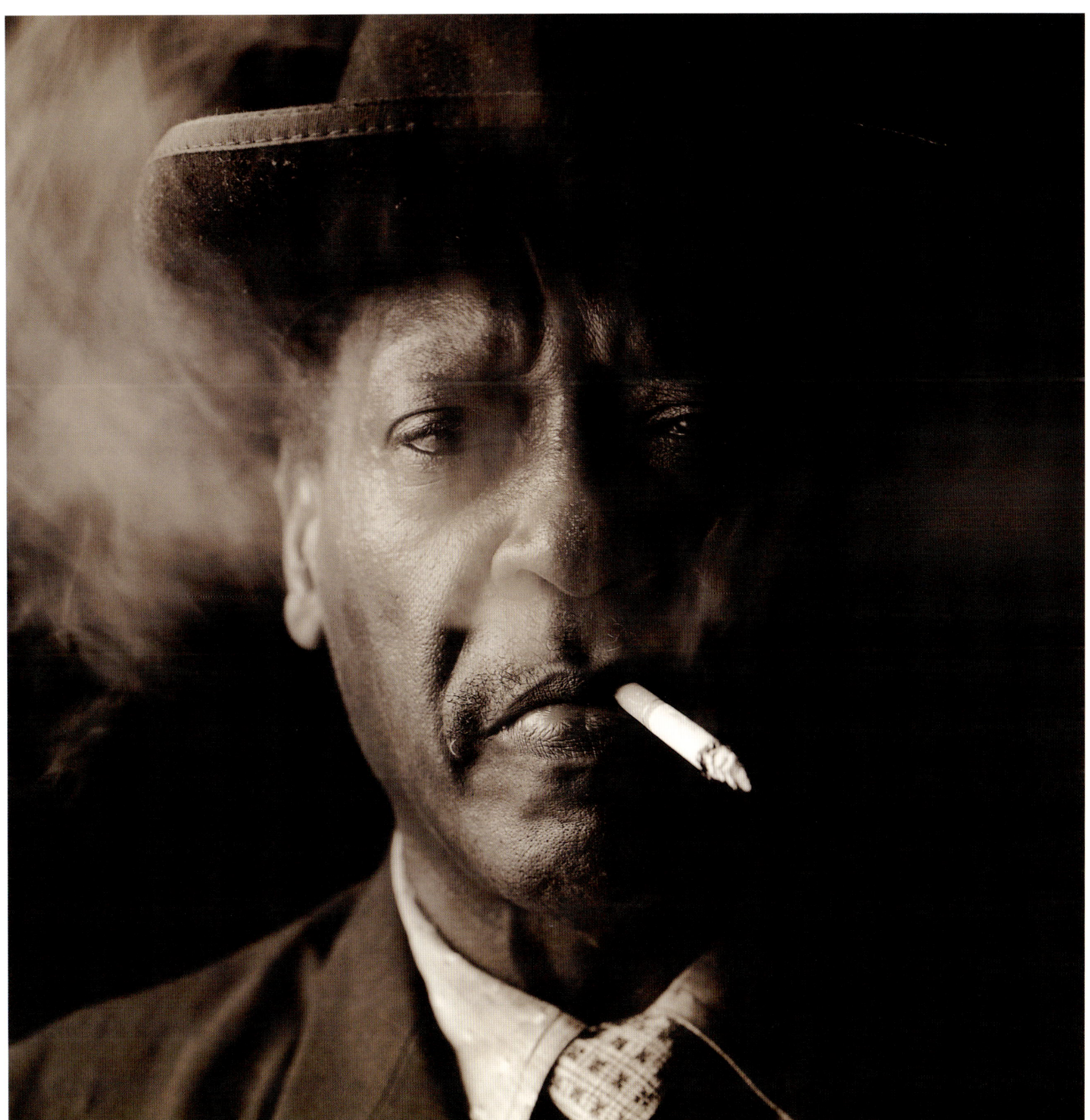

Eugene with Guitar. 1993, Greenville, Miss.

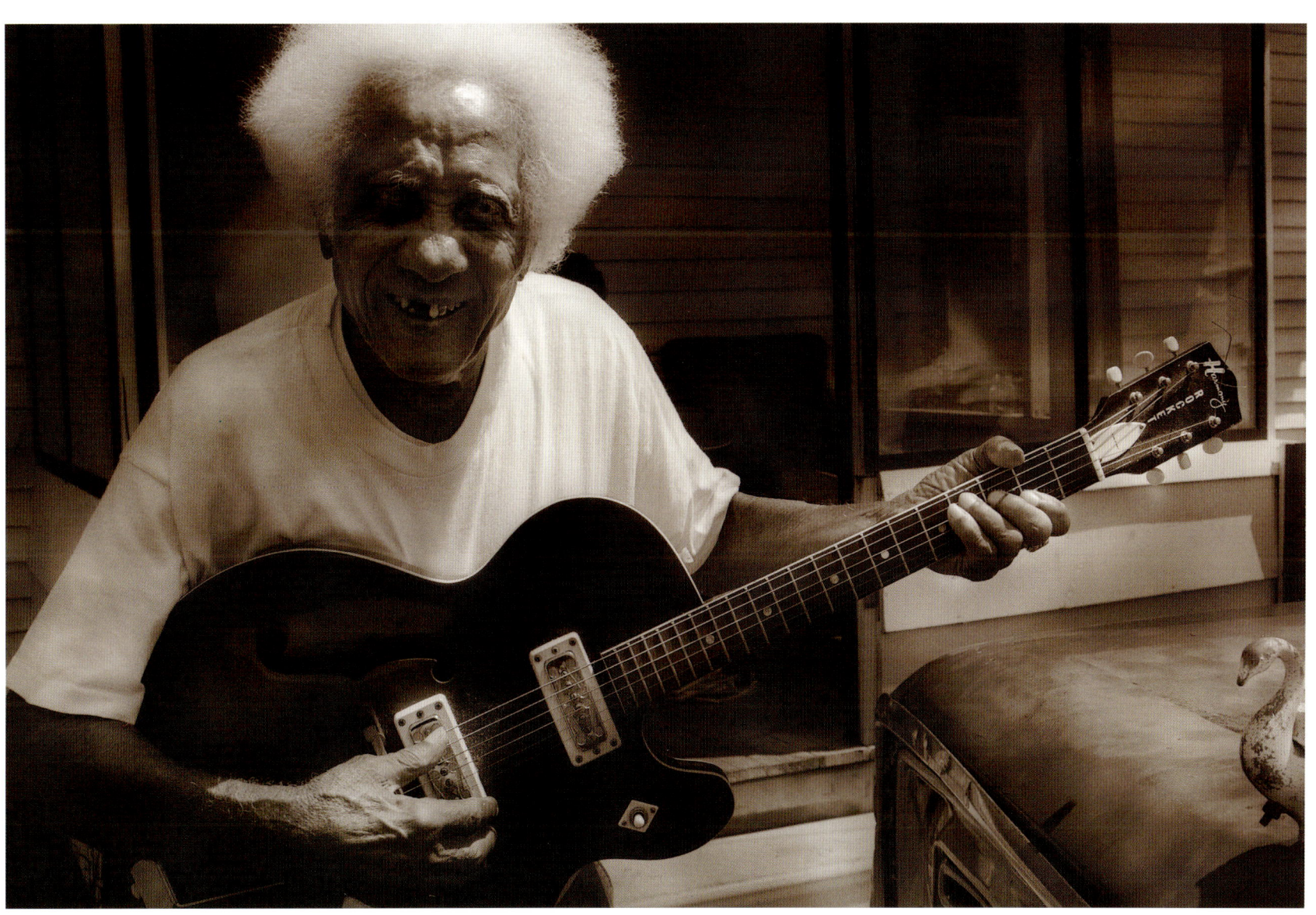

Eugene with Lois's Hand. 1993, Greenville, Miss.

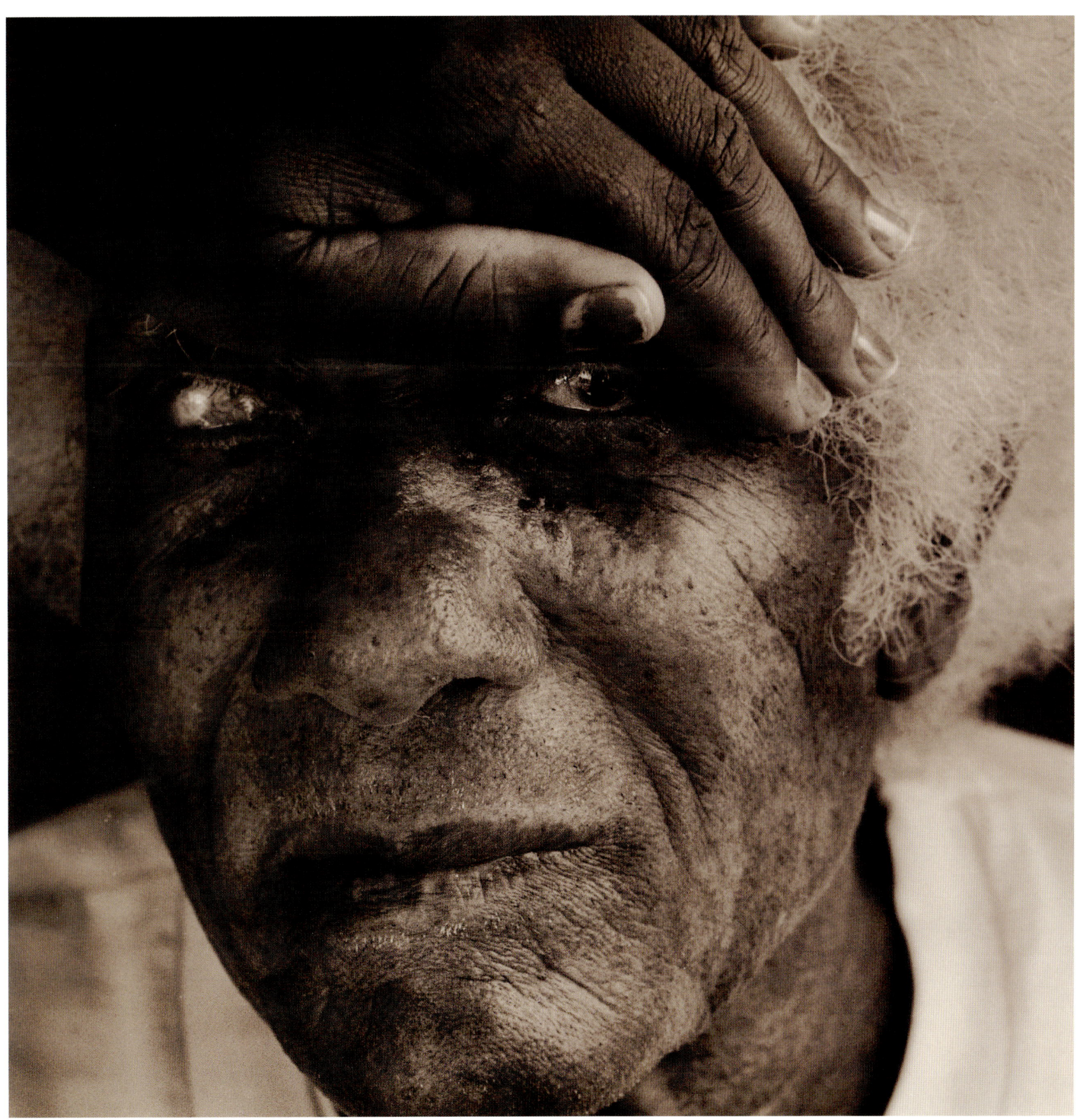

M. L. and Mr. Henry's Buick. 1997, Batesville, Miss.

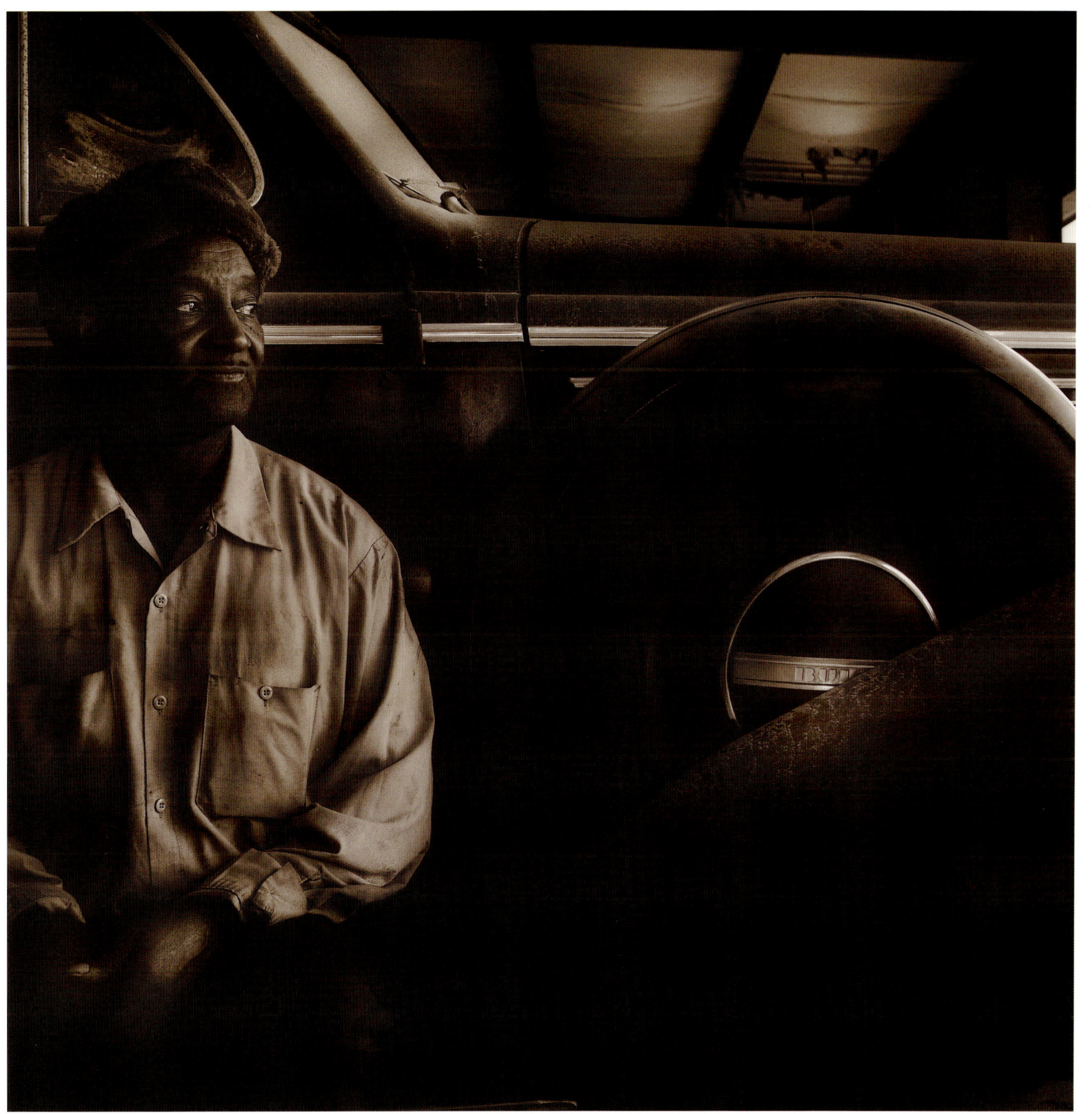

Dawn Fire. 1994, Coahoma County, Miss.

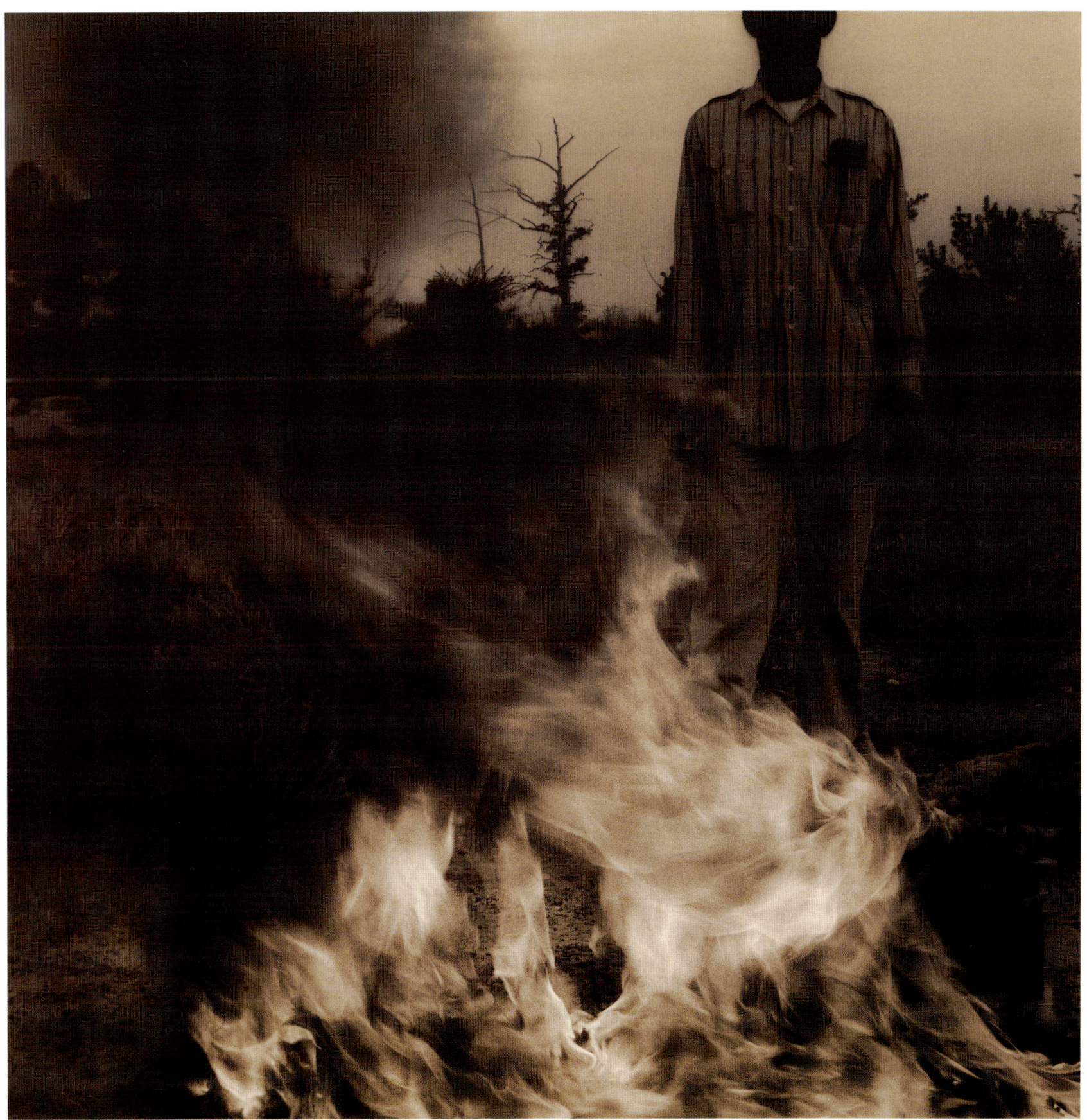

Field Burning No. 1. 1997, Russellville, Ala.

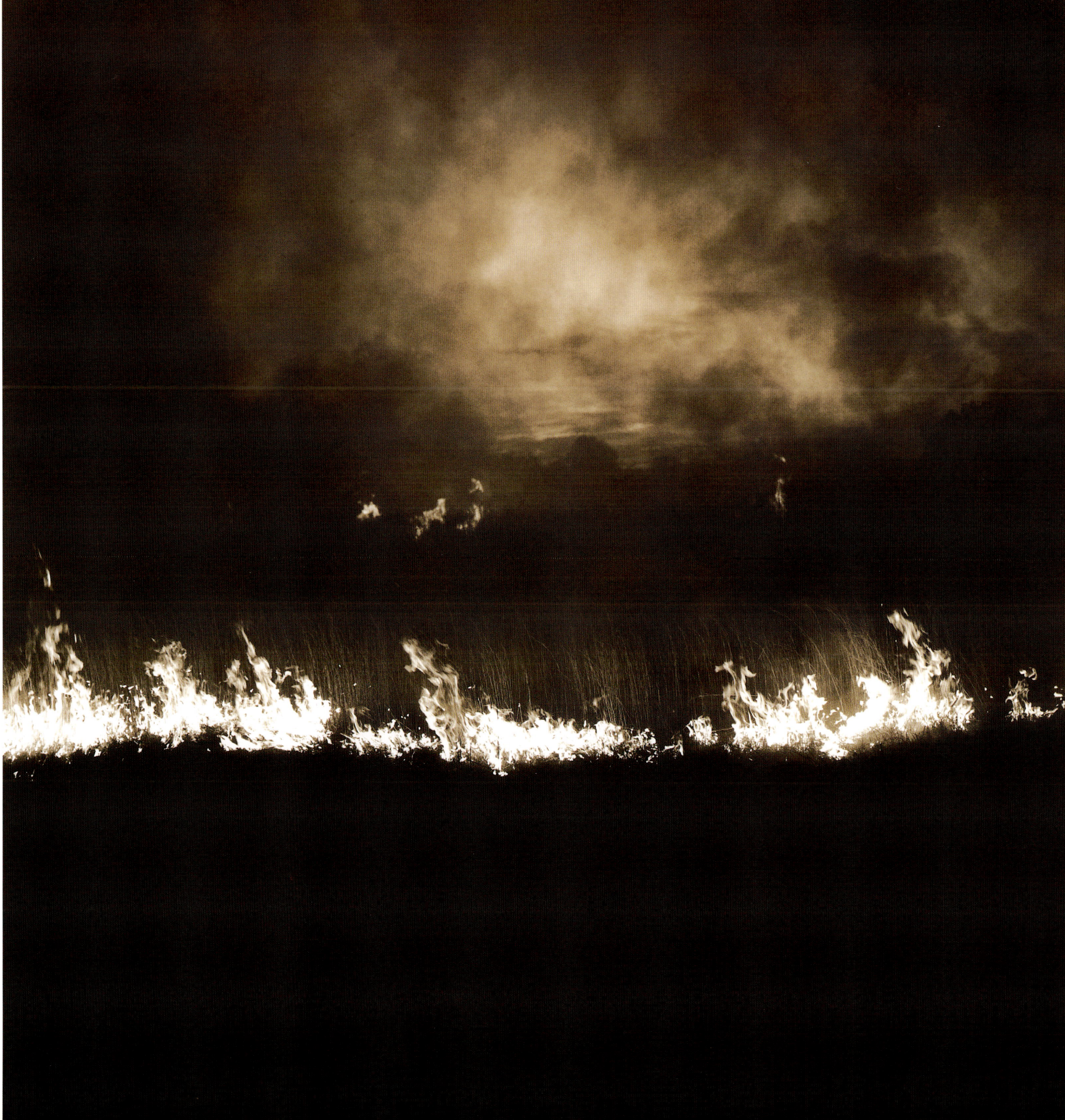

Man Sleeping in Pool.   1998, Savannah, Ga.

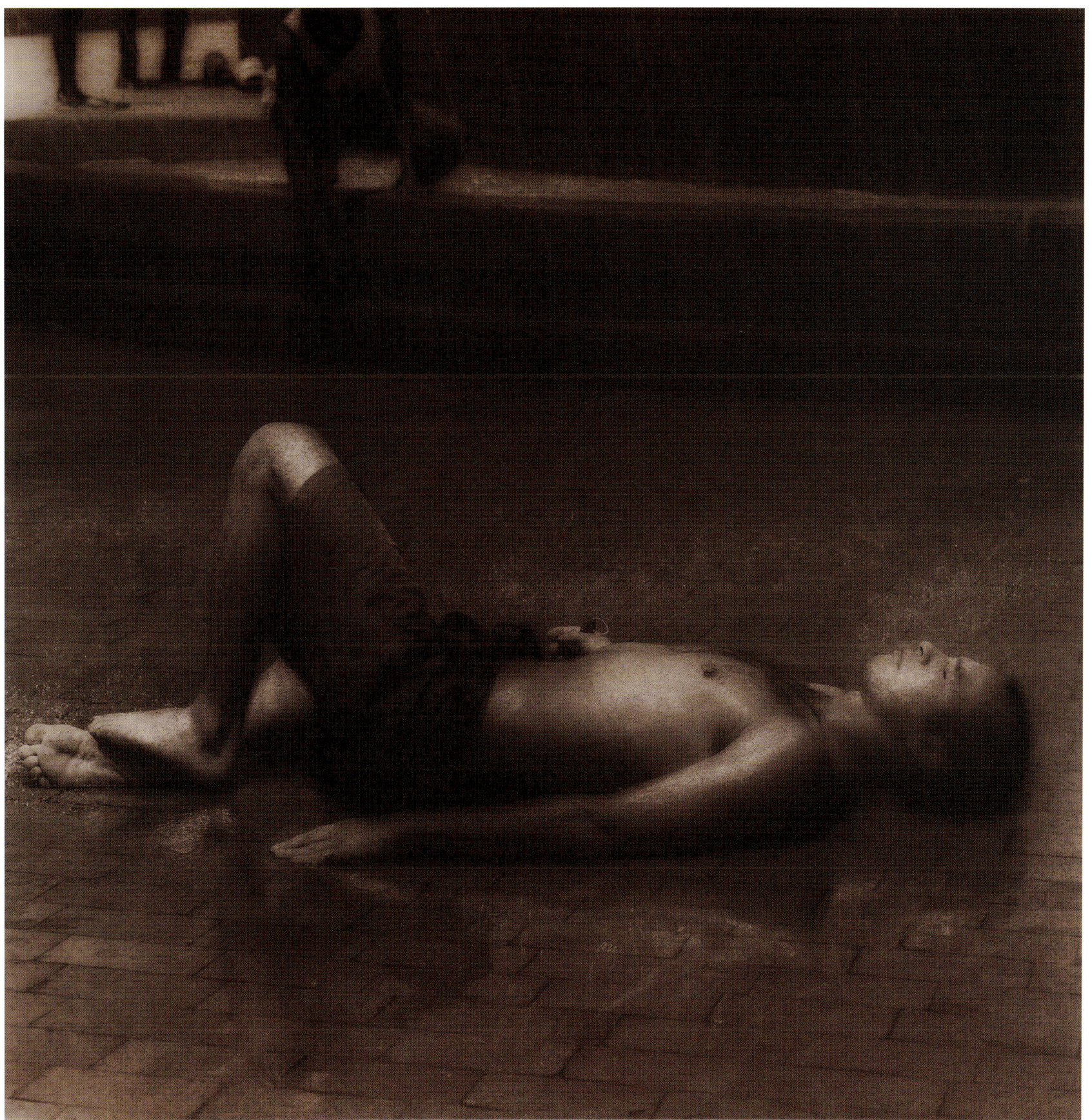

The Seiner. 1995, Le Flore County, Miss.

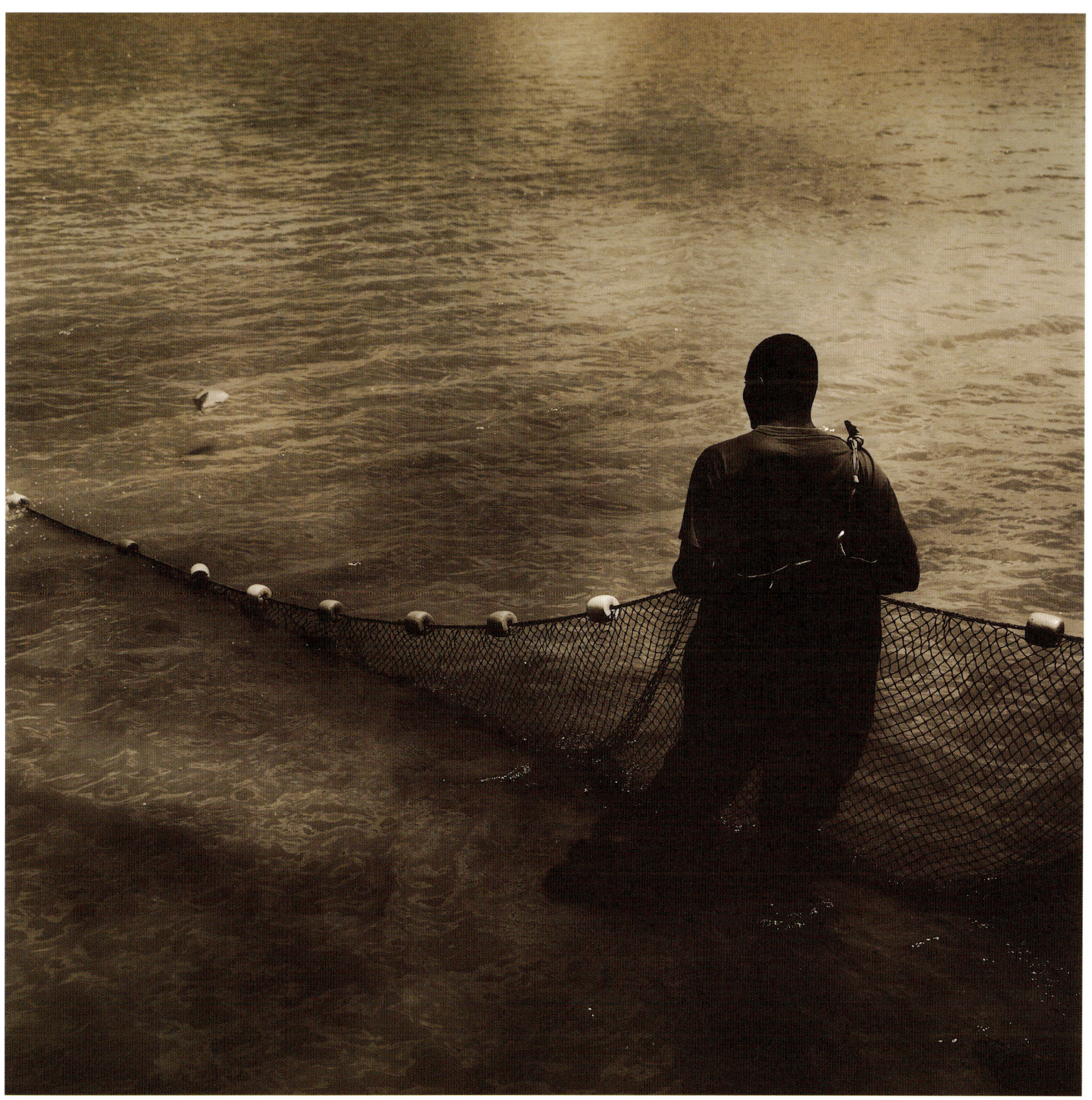

Merit Creek. 1995, Merit, Miss.

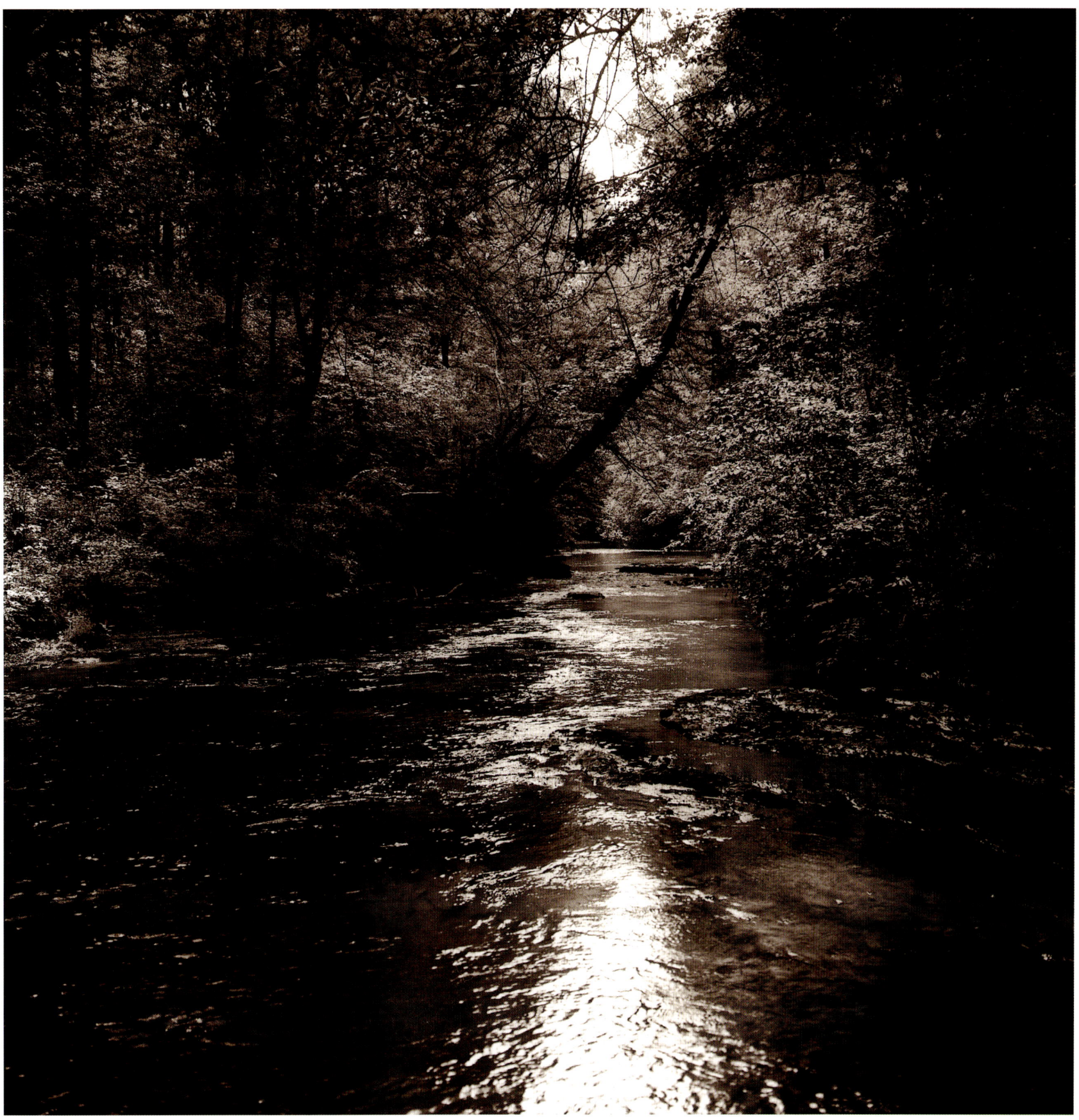

Rope Swing. 1994, Merit, Miss.

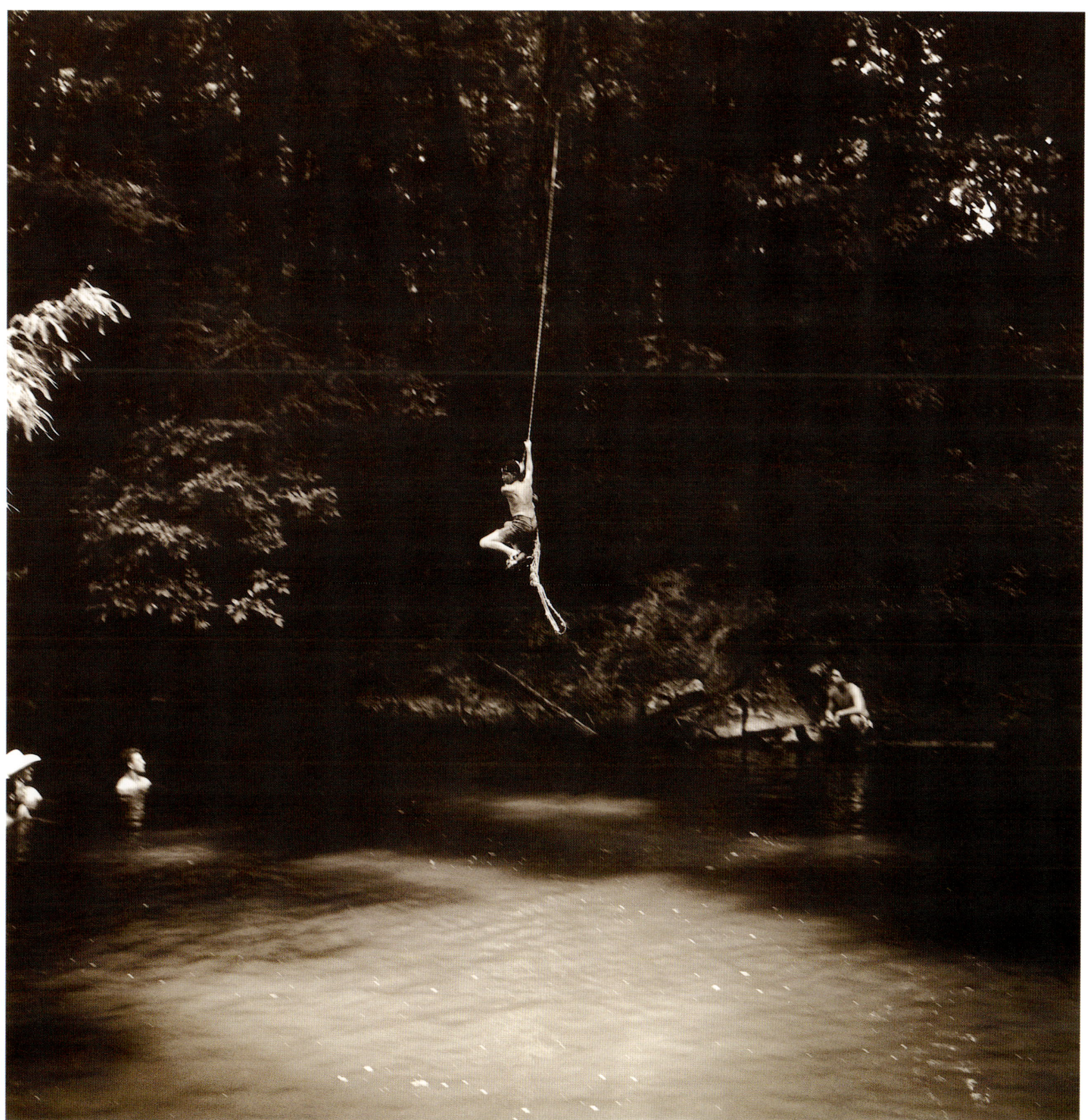

Diver. 1994, Merit, Miss.

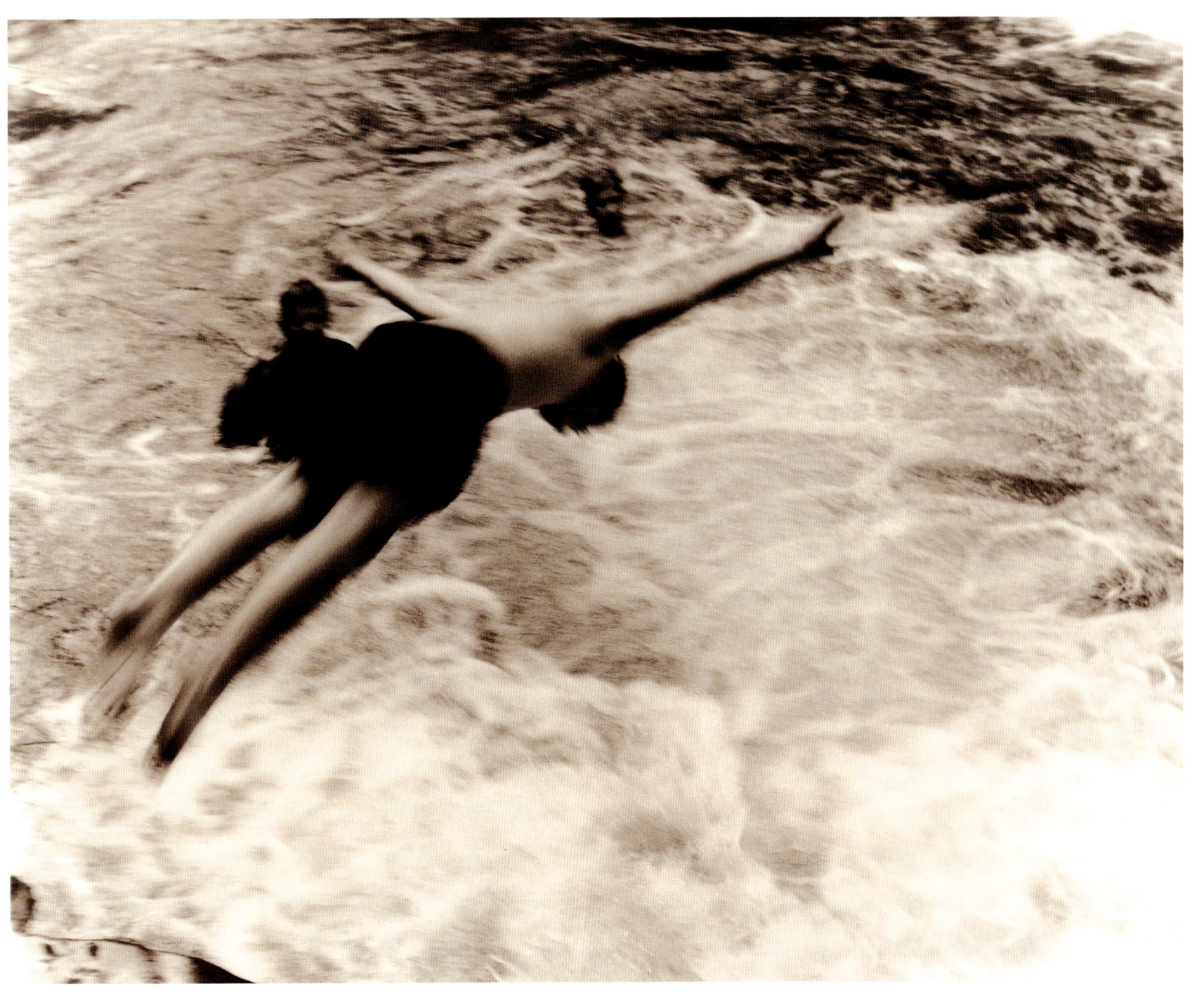

SWIMMER. 1994, McComb, Miss.

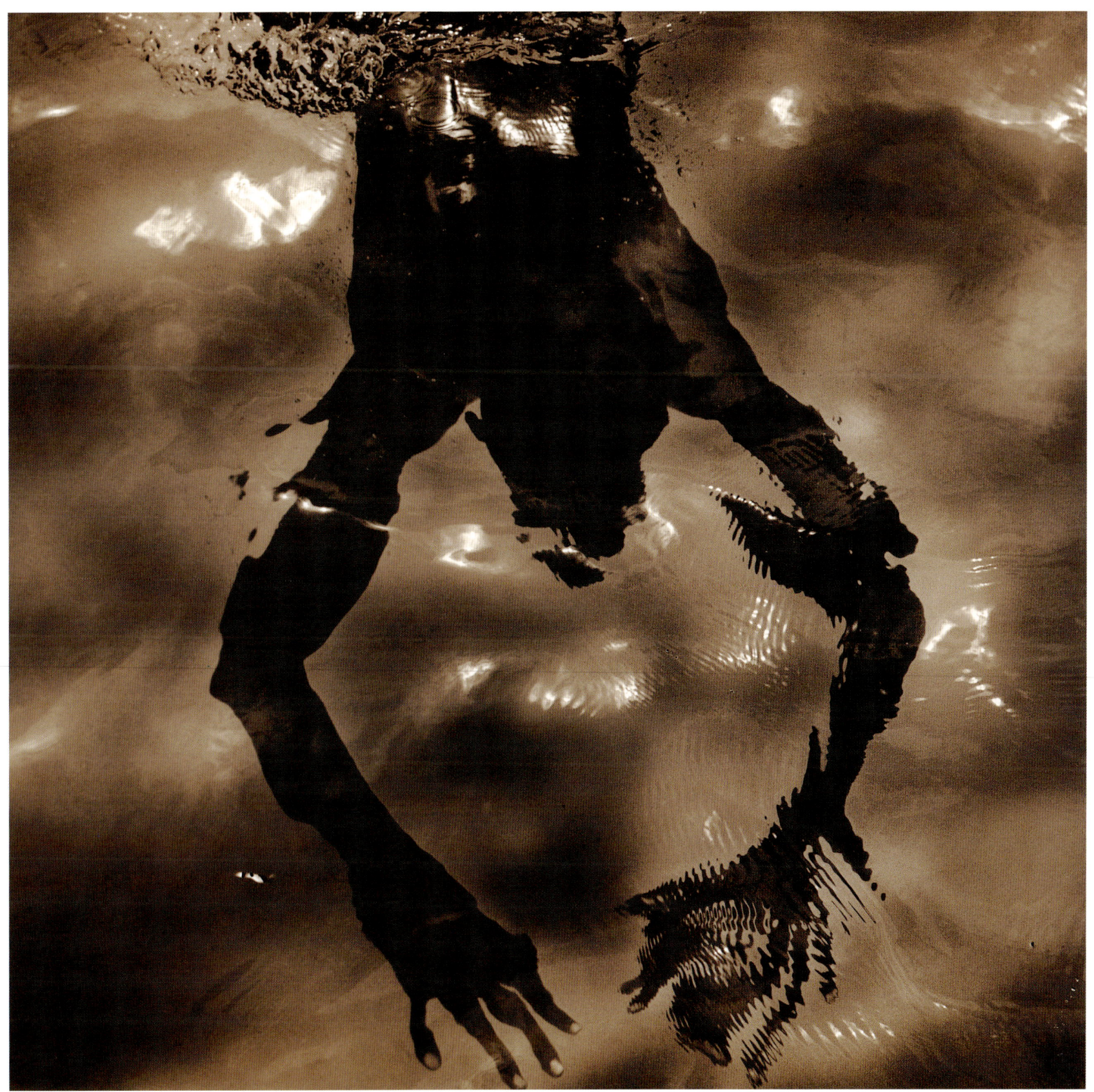

WATERDOGS. 1998, New Orleans.

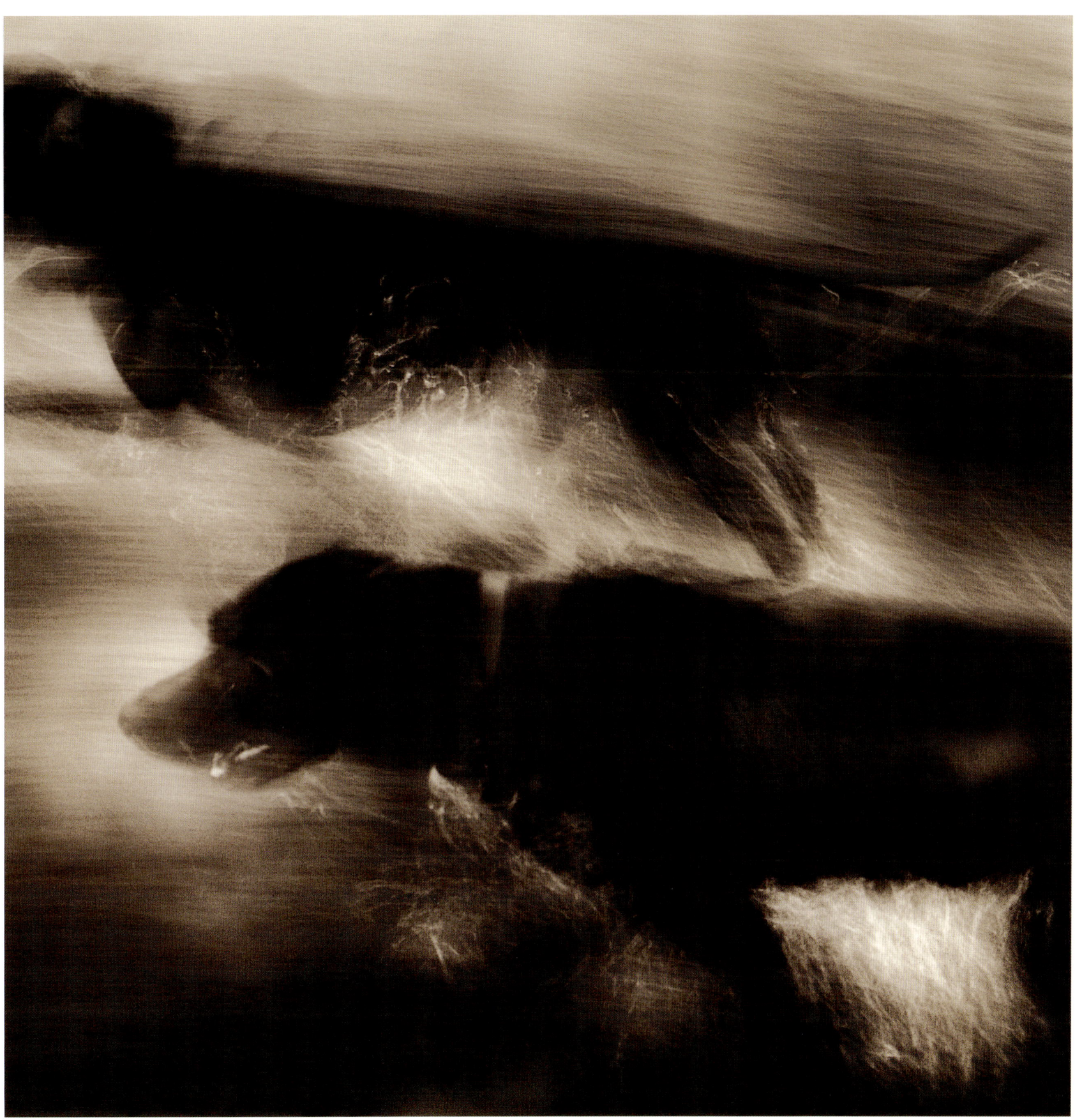

Lake Pontchartrain. 1997, Mandeville, La.

Composition at Josephine's. 1998, New Orleans.

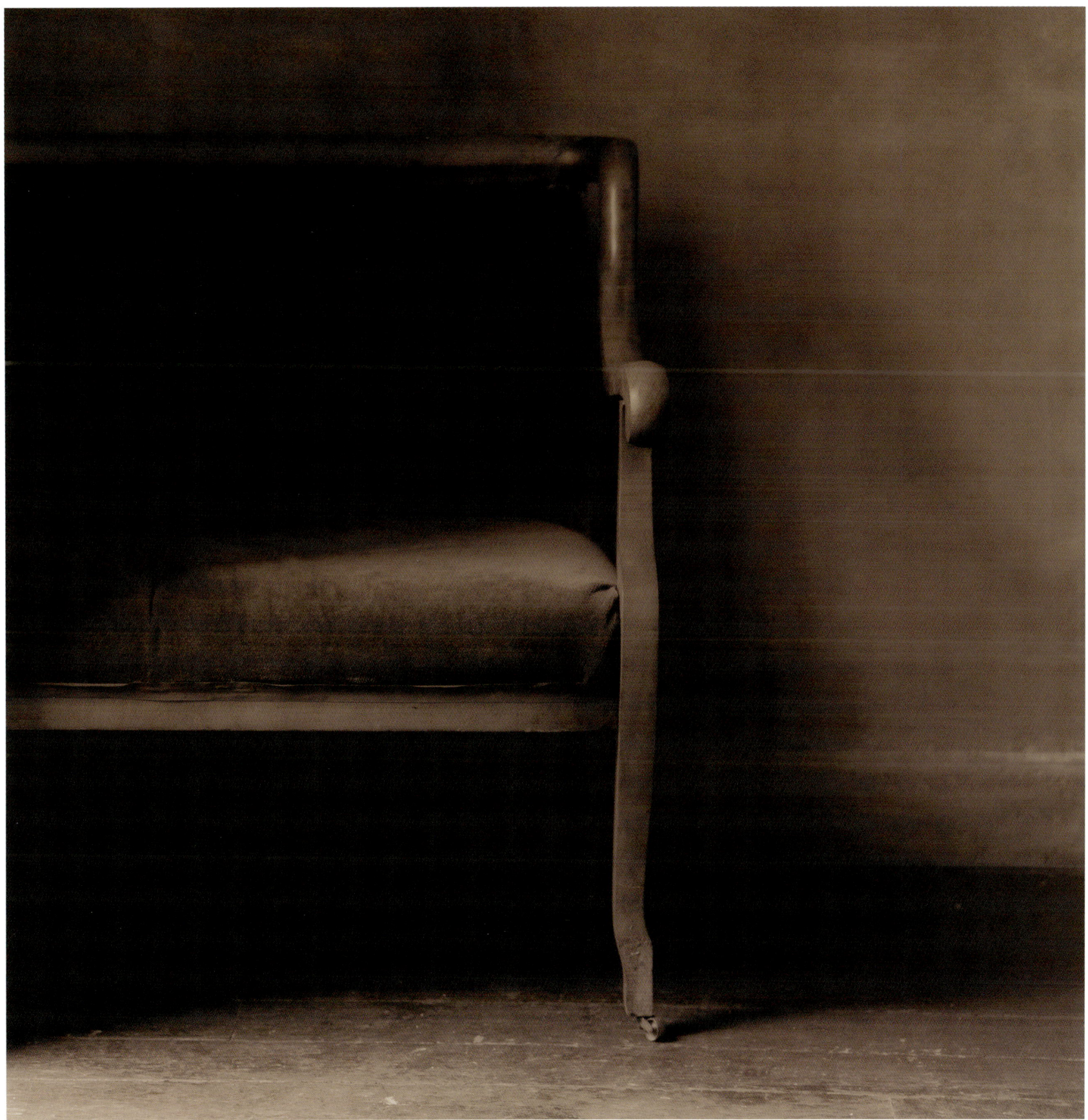

Kate's Nocturne. 1998, Jackson, Miss.

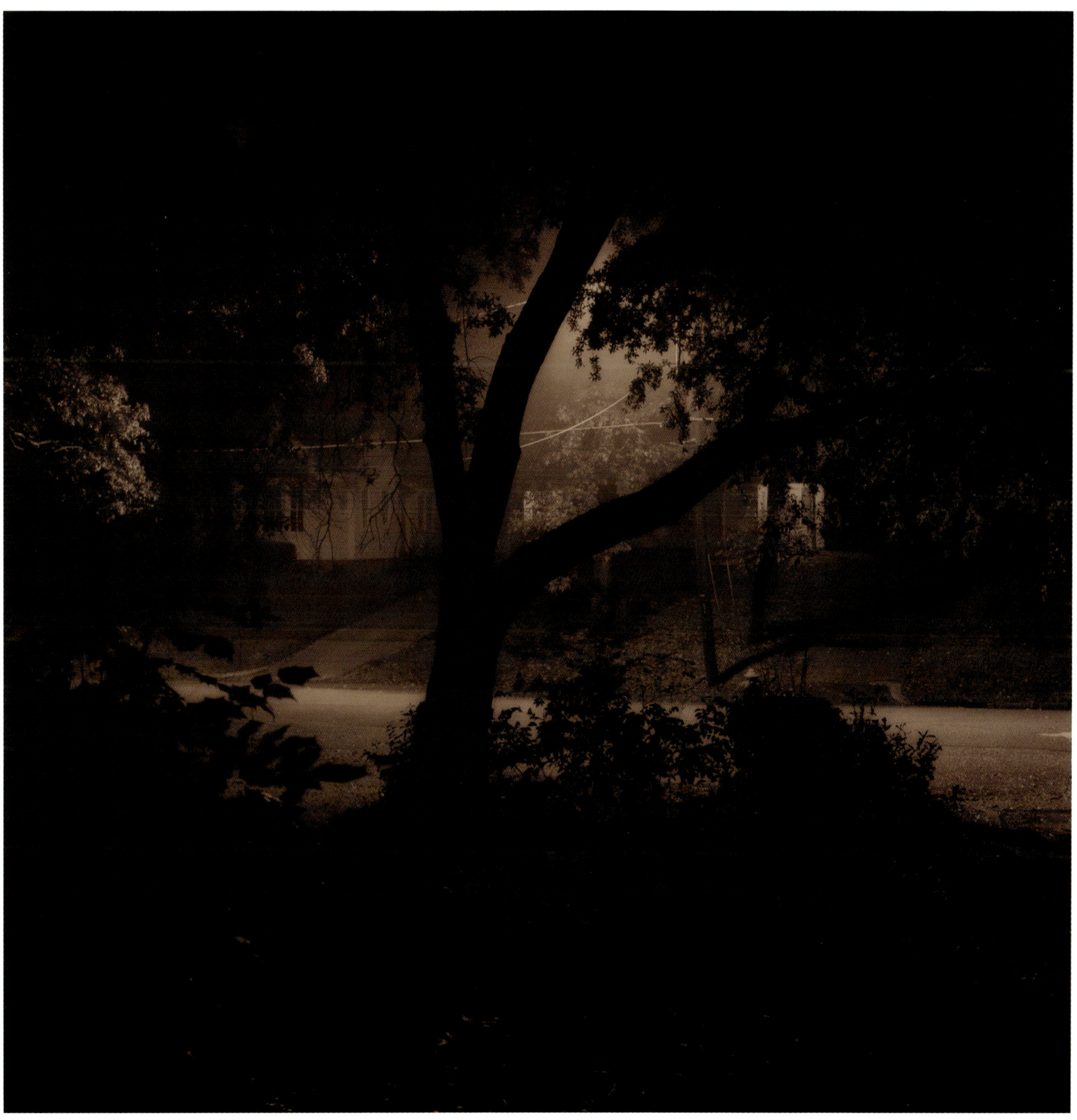

Kate in the Streetlight. 1998, Jackson, Miss.

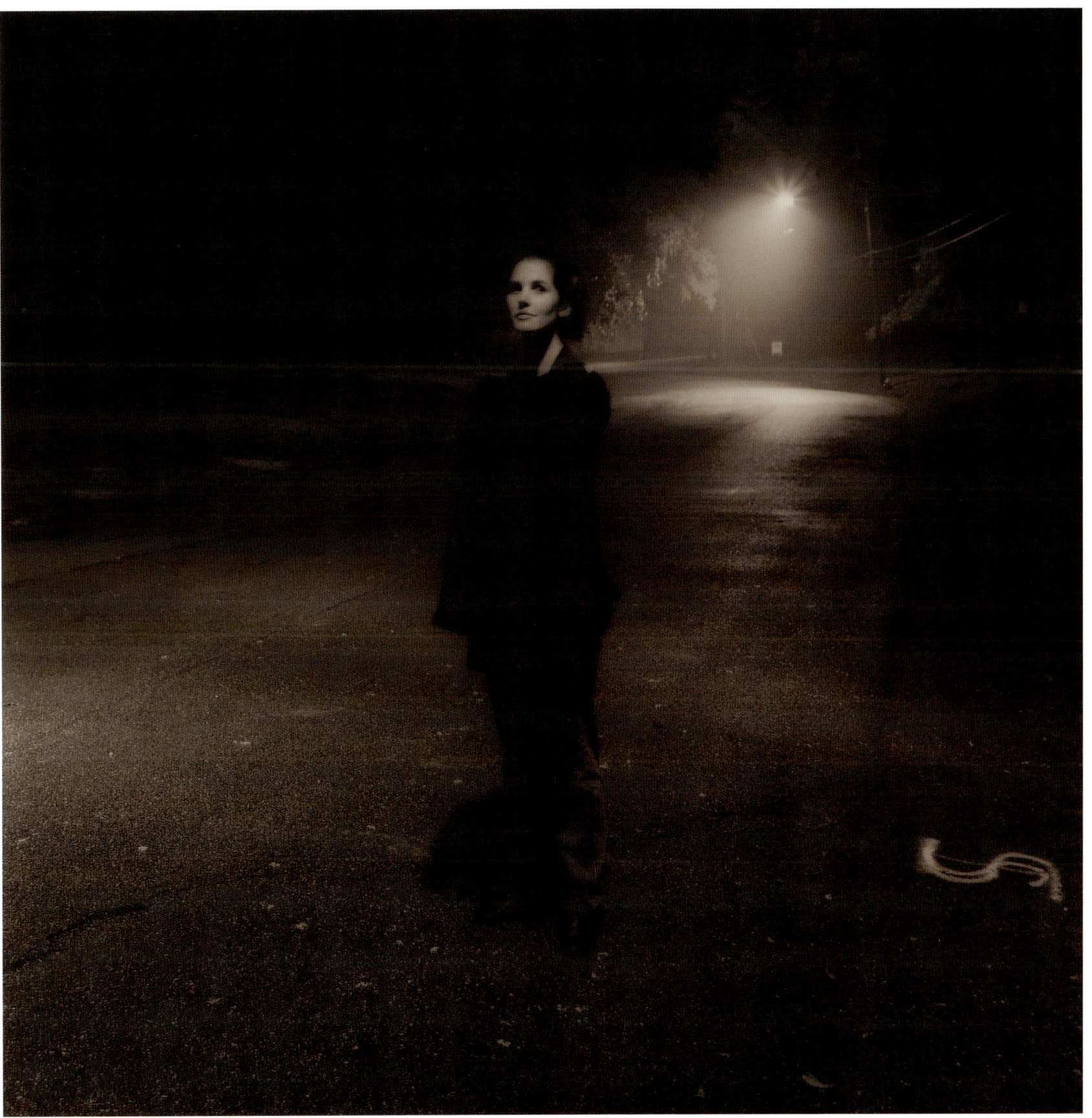

Oxford Nocturne. 1996, Oxford, Miss.

Overleaf:
Bridge over Bayou Teche. 1996, Breaux Bridge, La.
Bayou Teche. 1996, Breaux Bridge, La.

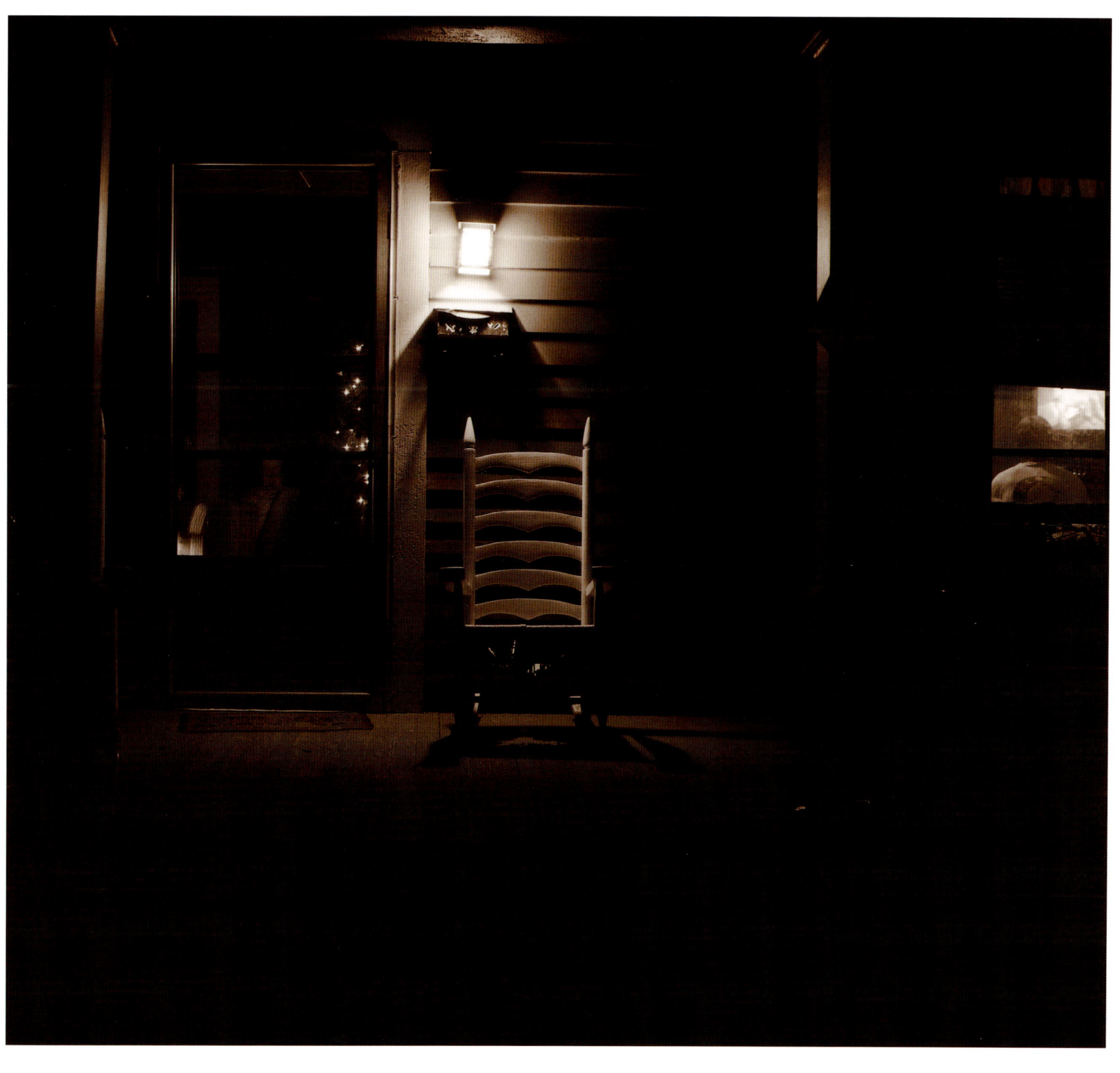

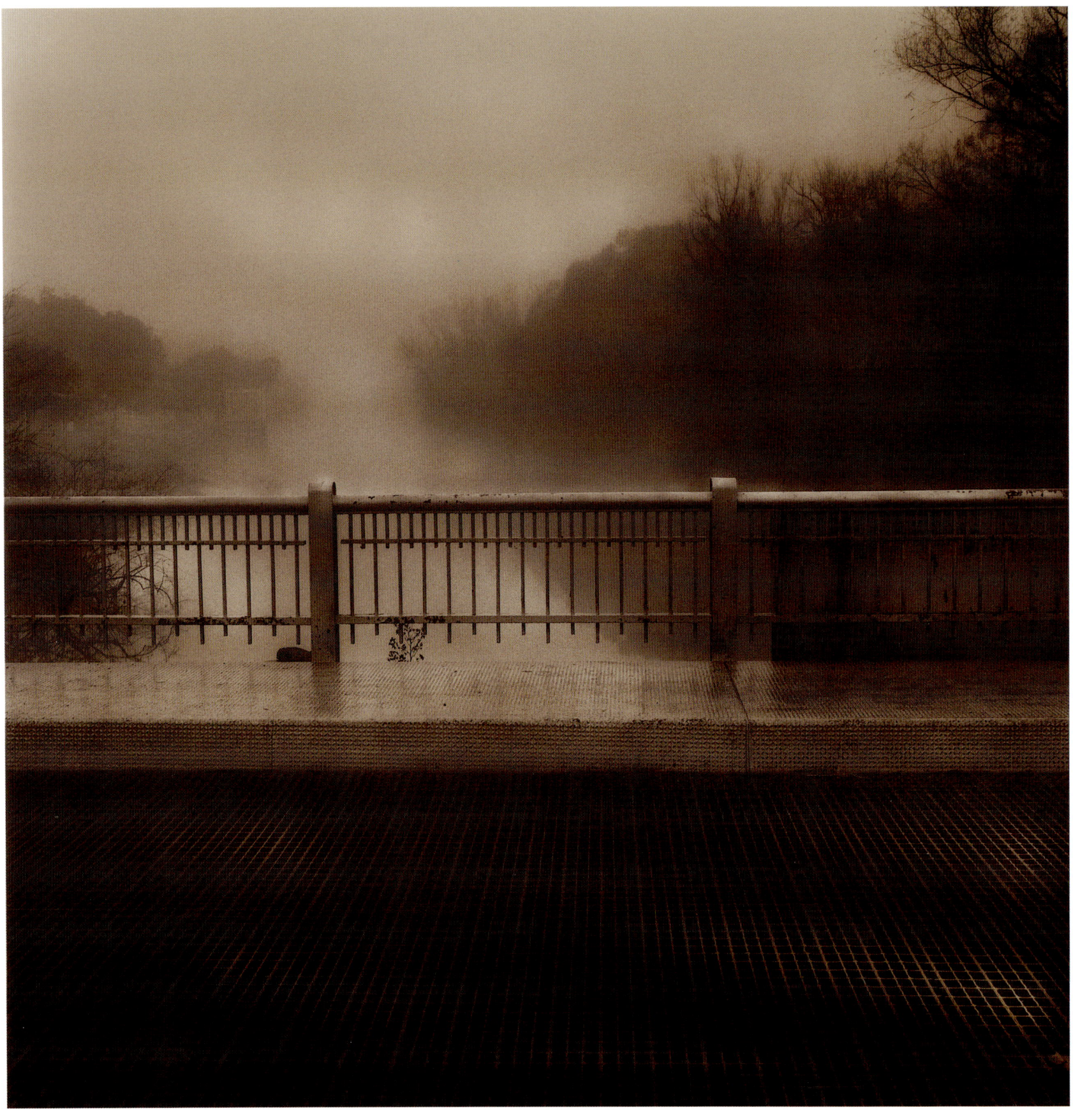

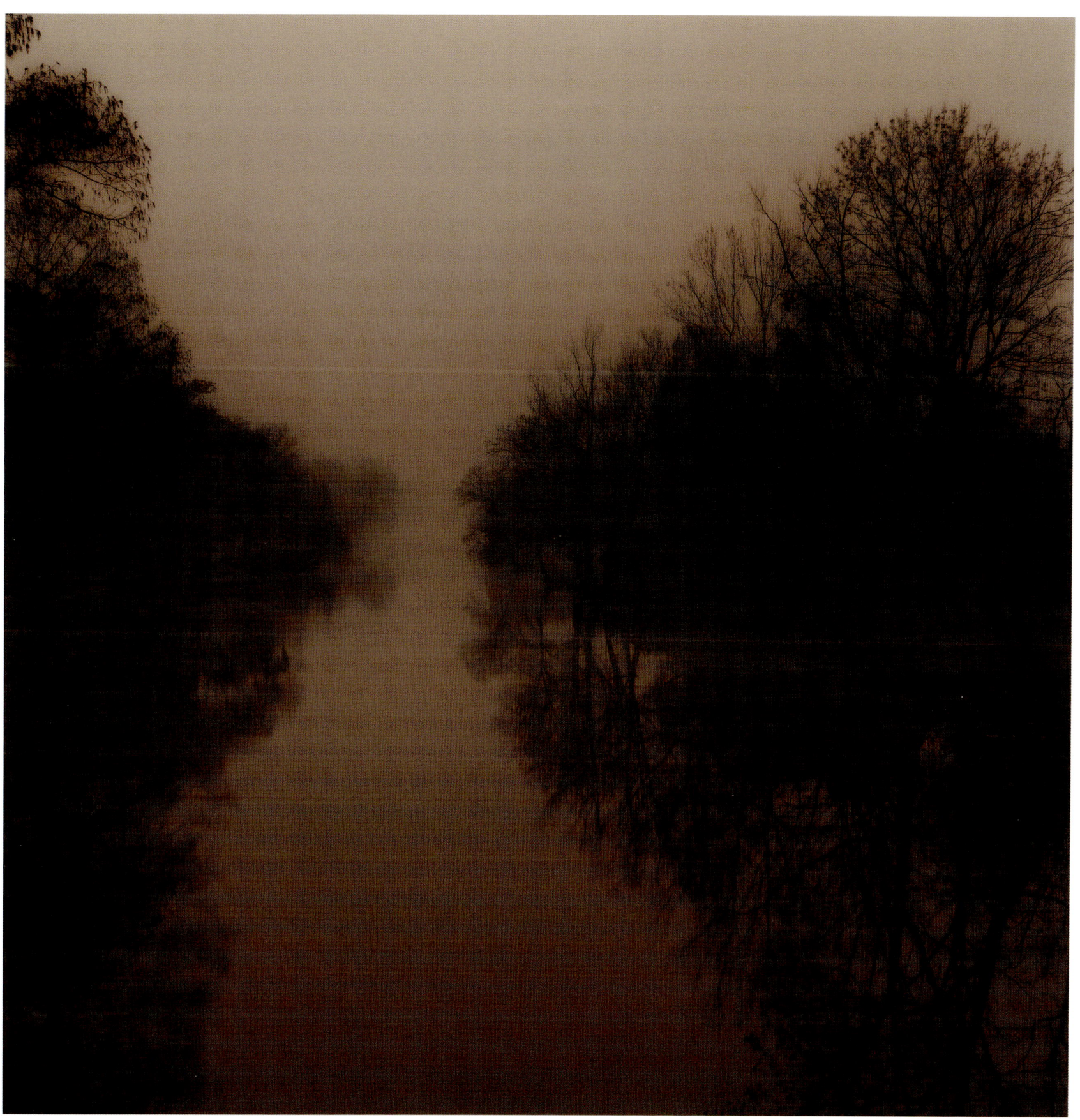

Dead Tree. 1998, Fripp Island, S.C.

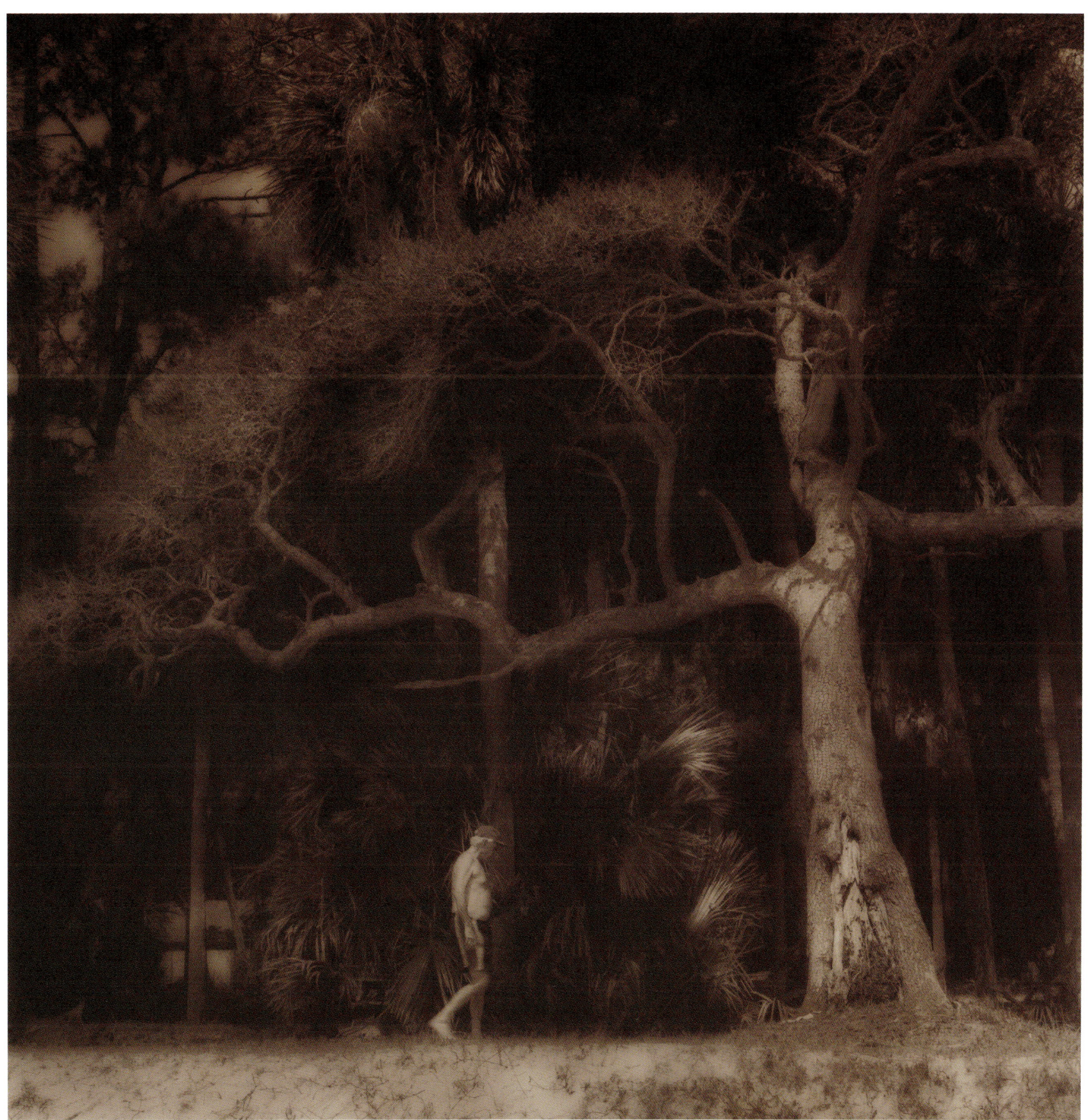

January, Panther Burn. 1992, Panther Burn, Miss.

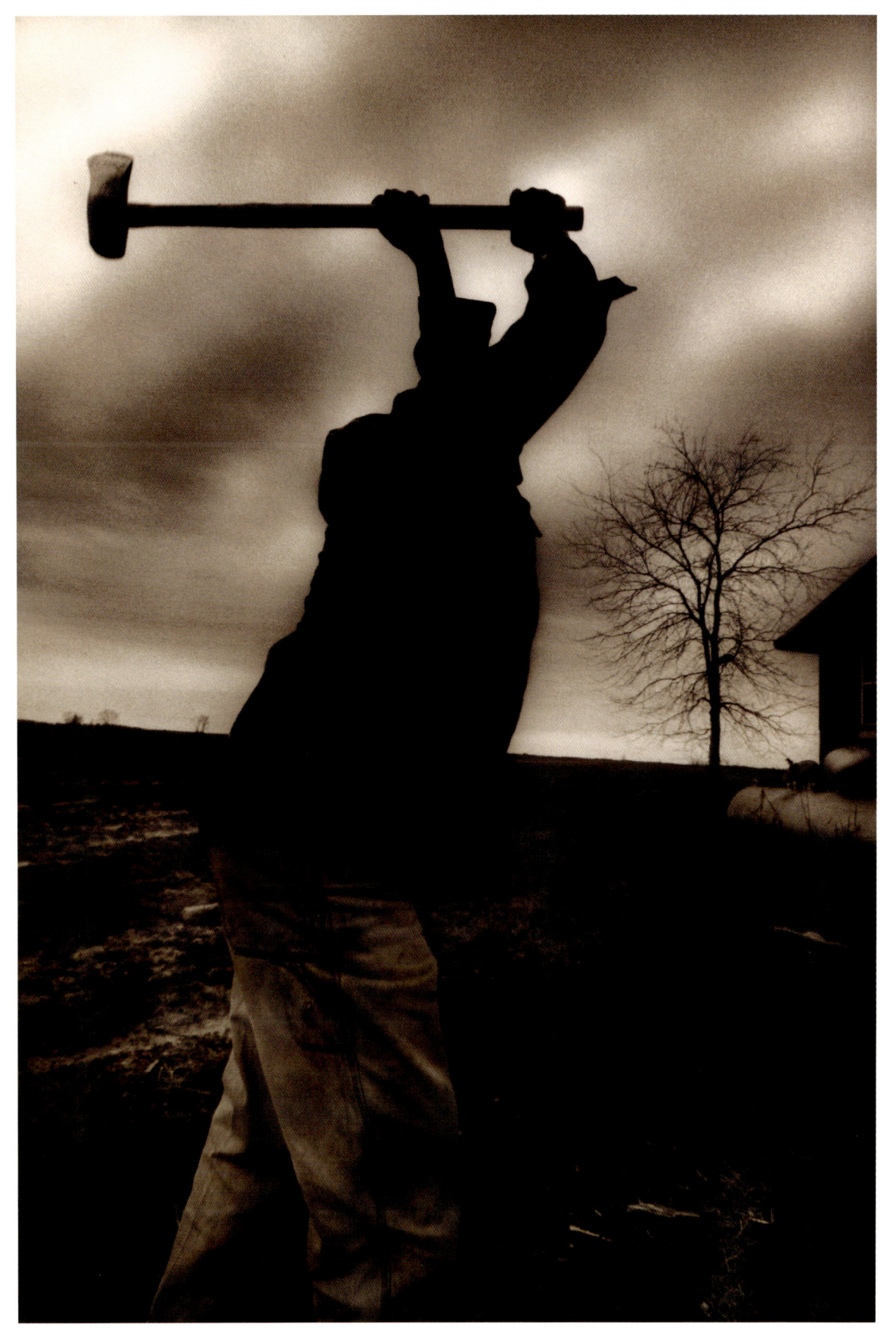

Mr. Will. 1994, Merigold, Miss.

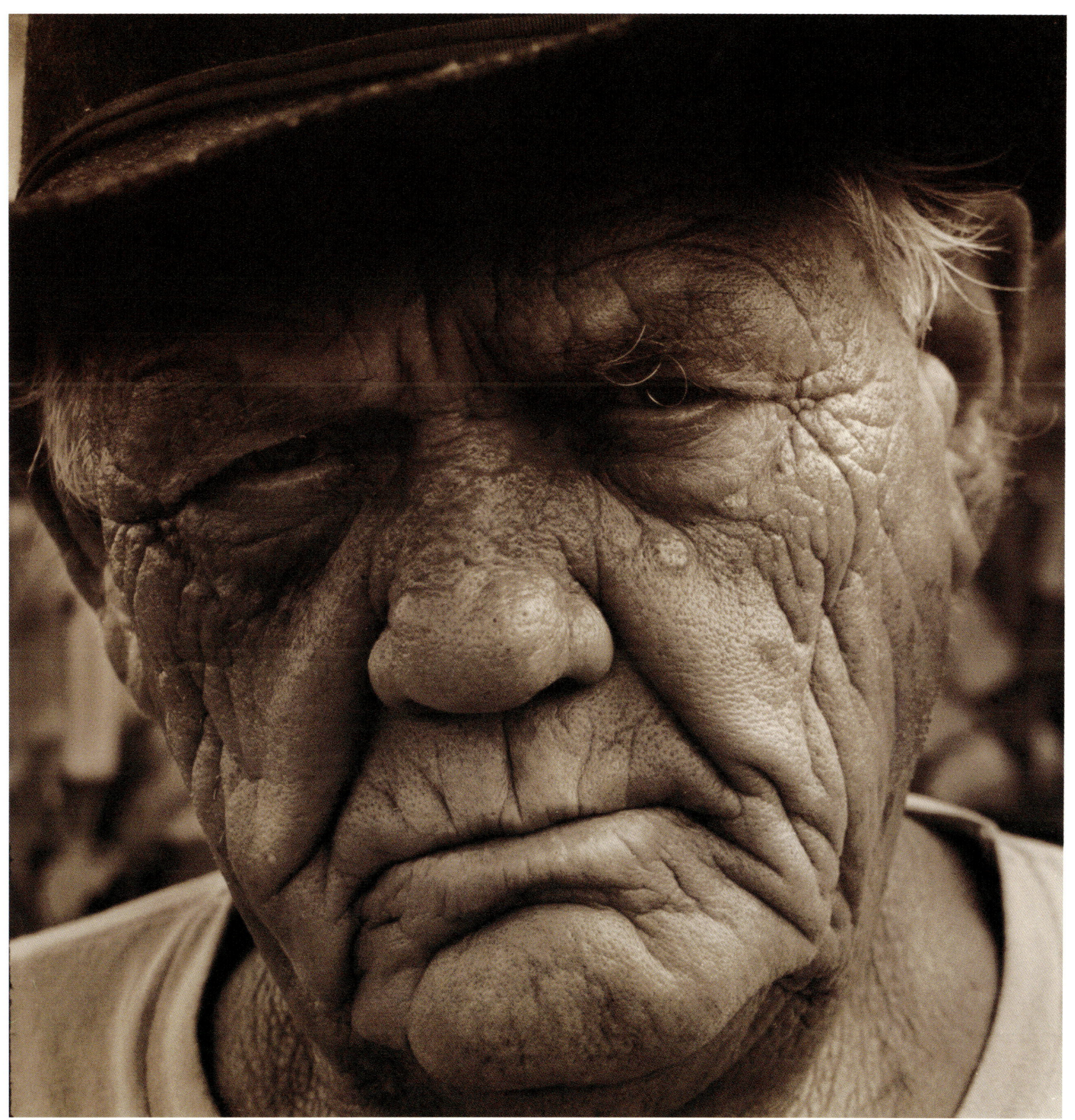

Mr. Will at the Barber Shop. 1994, Merigold, Miss.

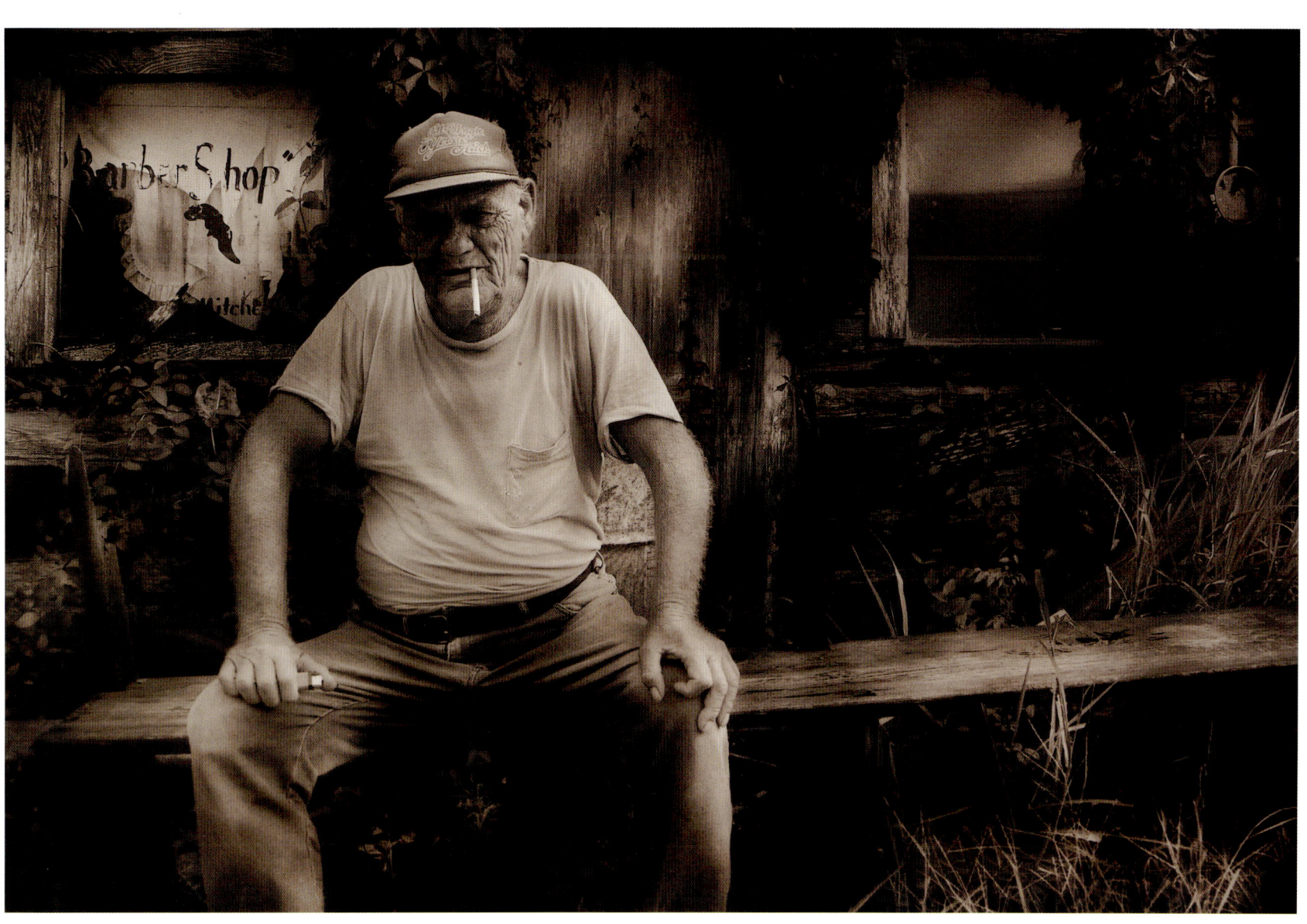

Snake Killer. 1994, Blackhawk, Miss.

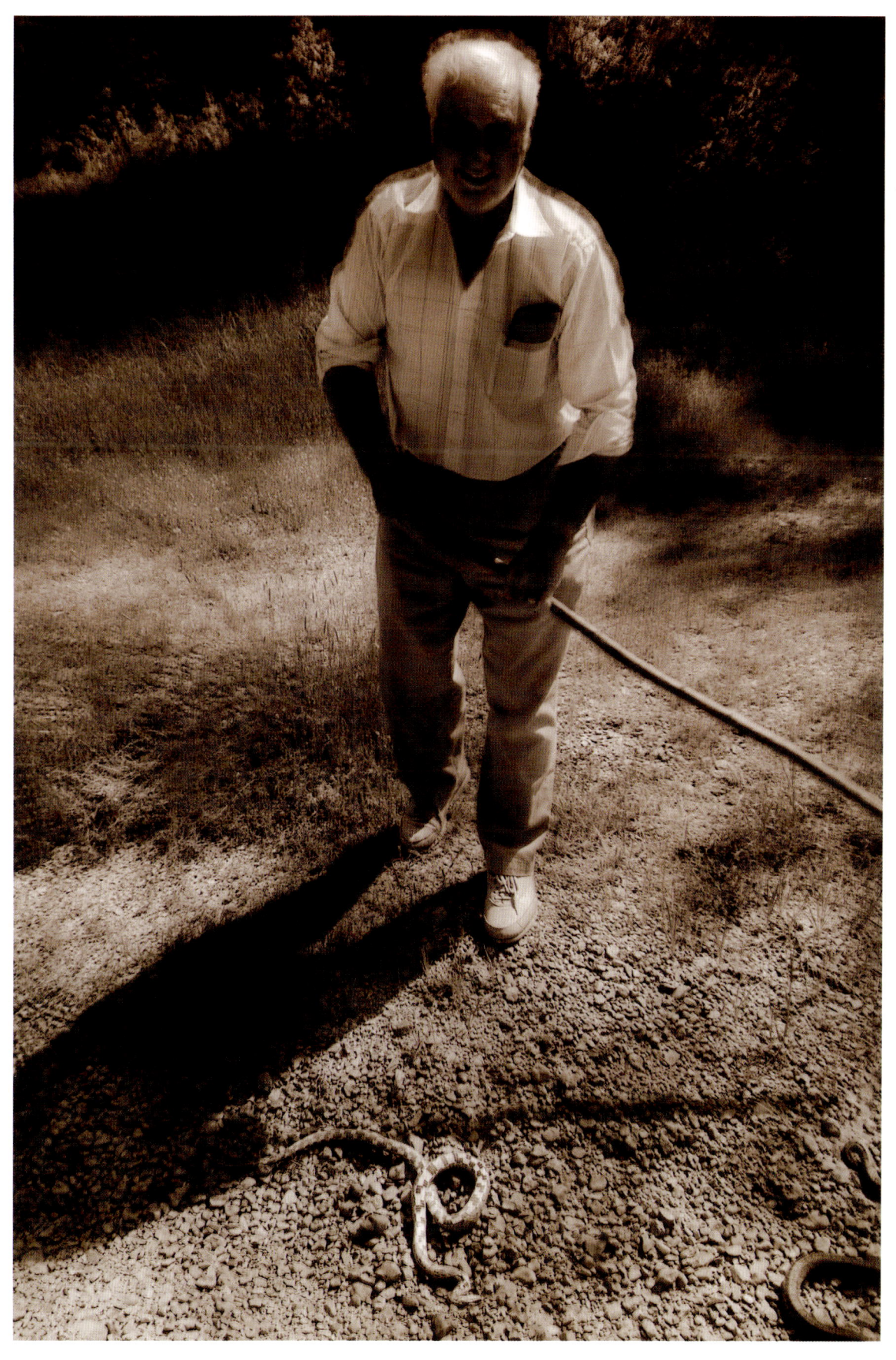

HAND ON DOOR SCREEN. 1998, Coila, Miss.

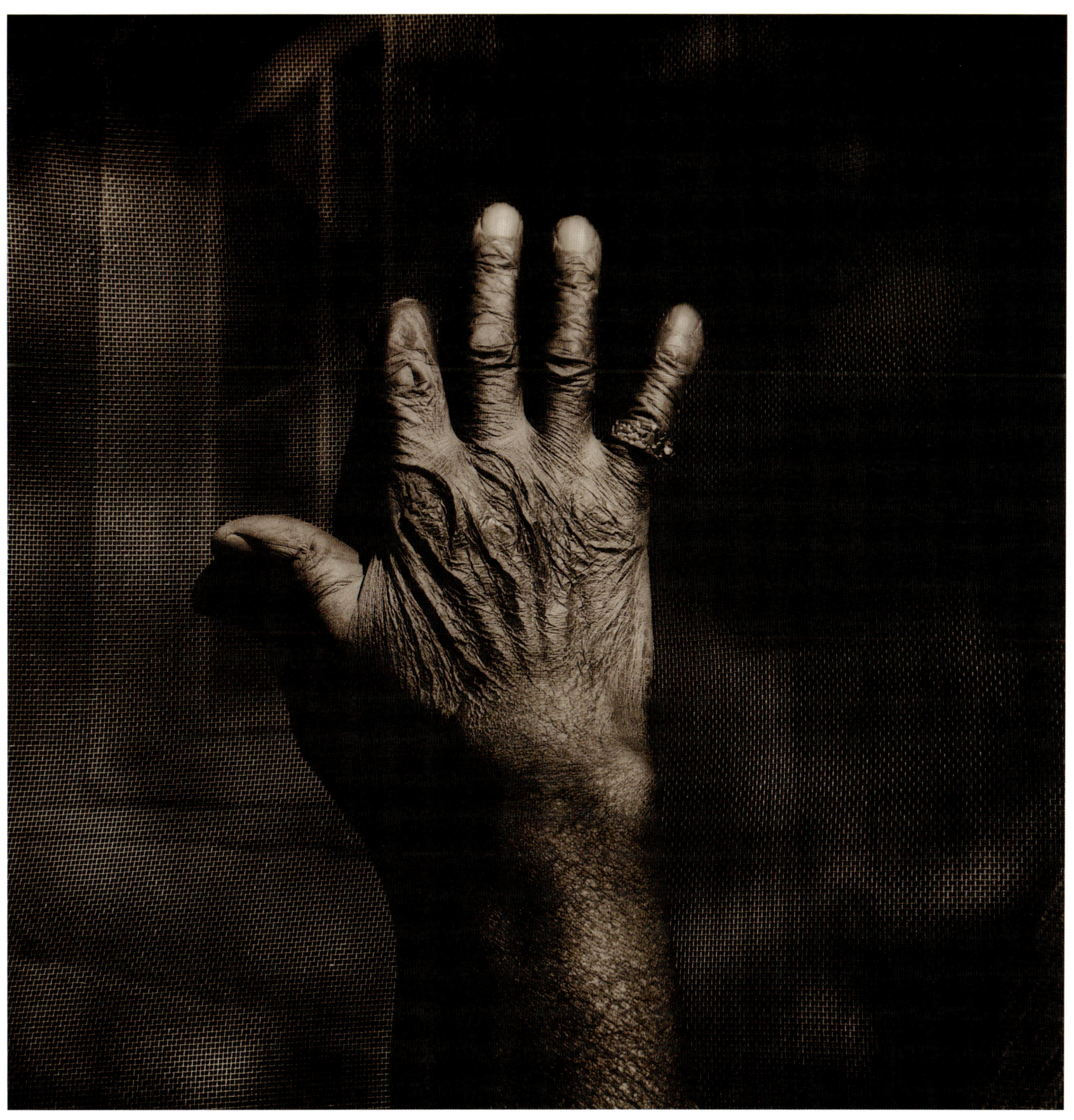

Alex. 1990, England, Ark.

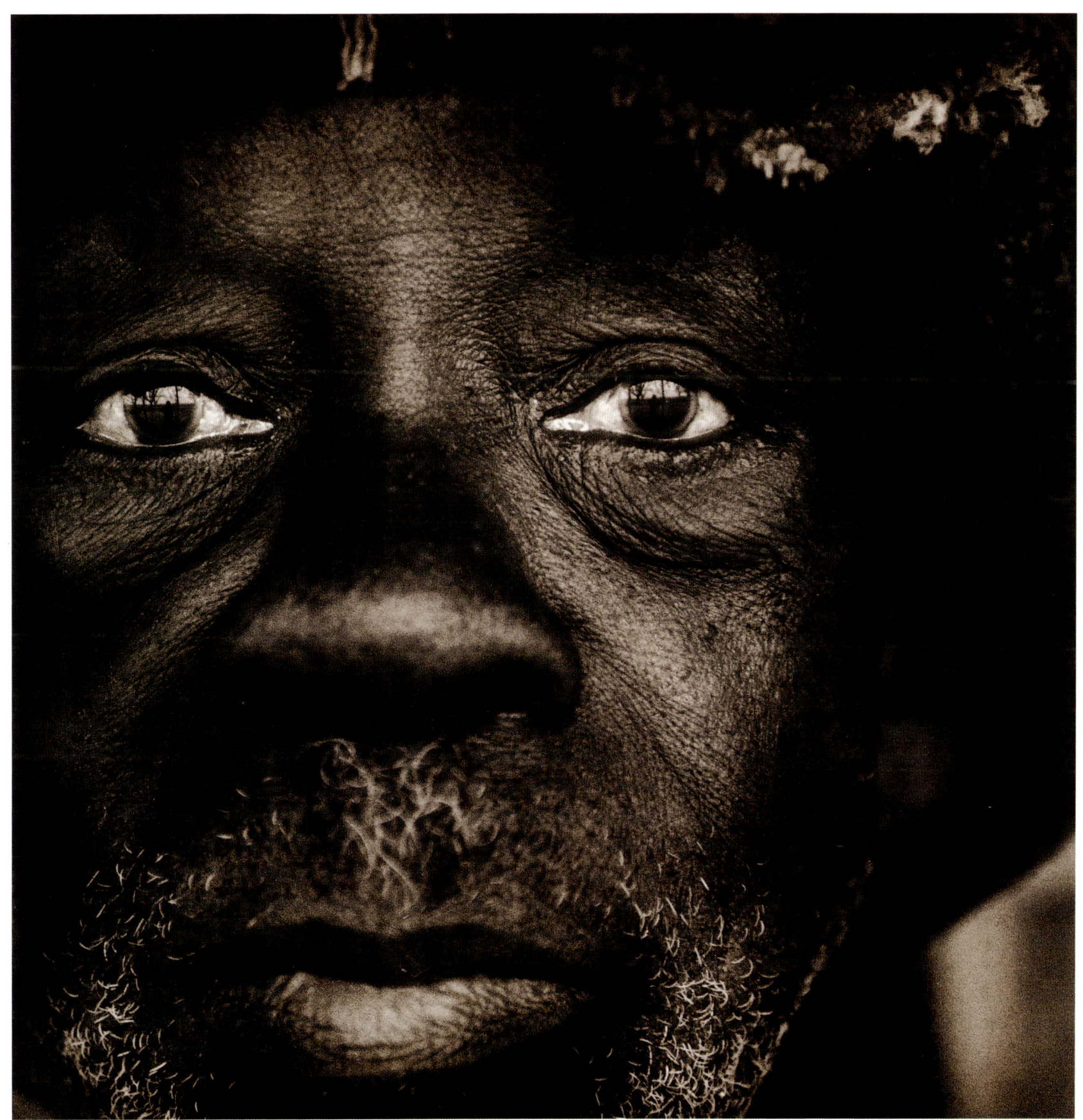

Alex at Home. 1990, England, Ark.

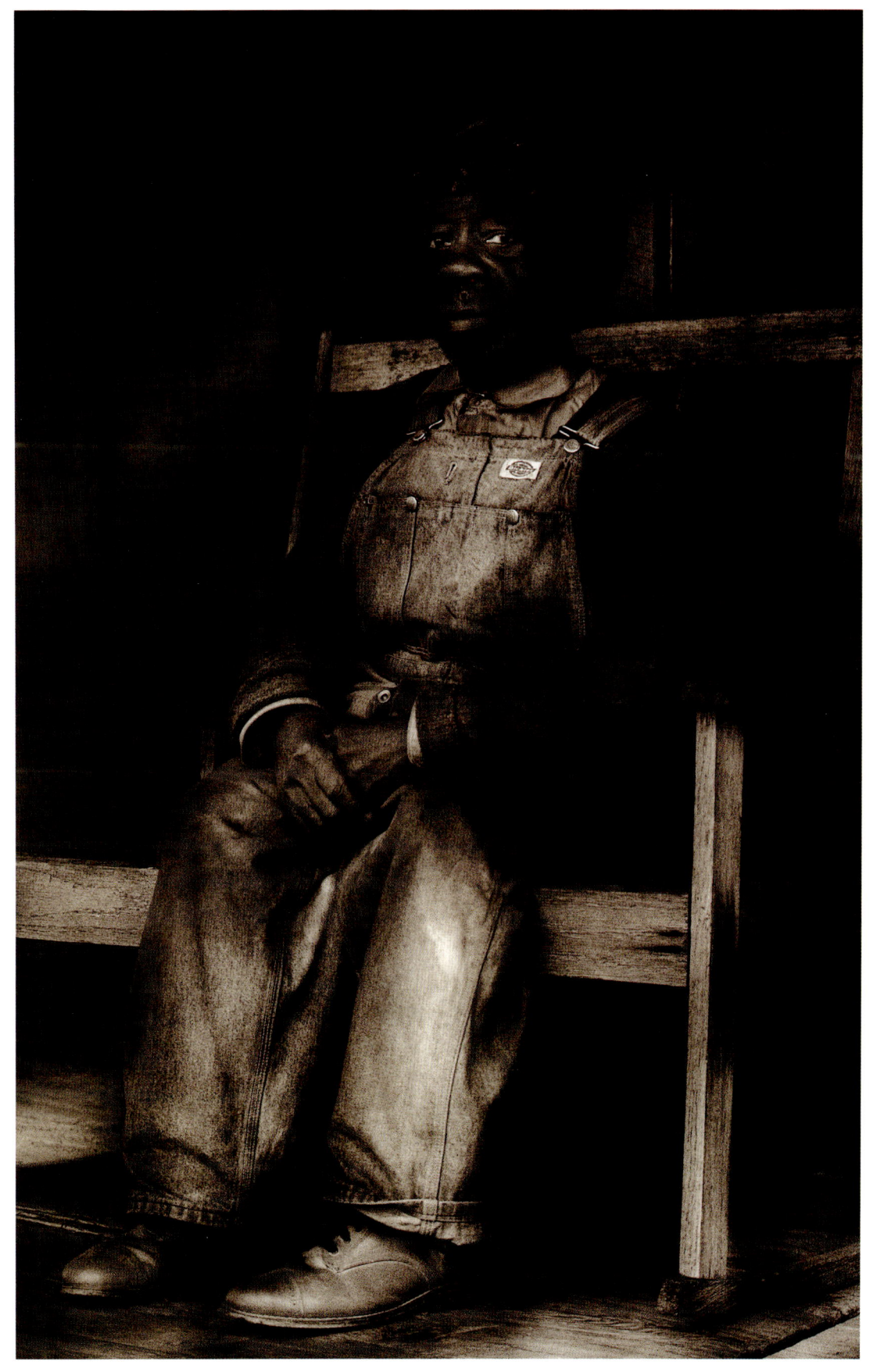

Mr. Bihm and Sons. 1998, Palmetto, La.

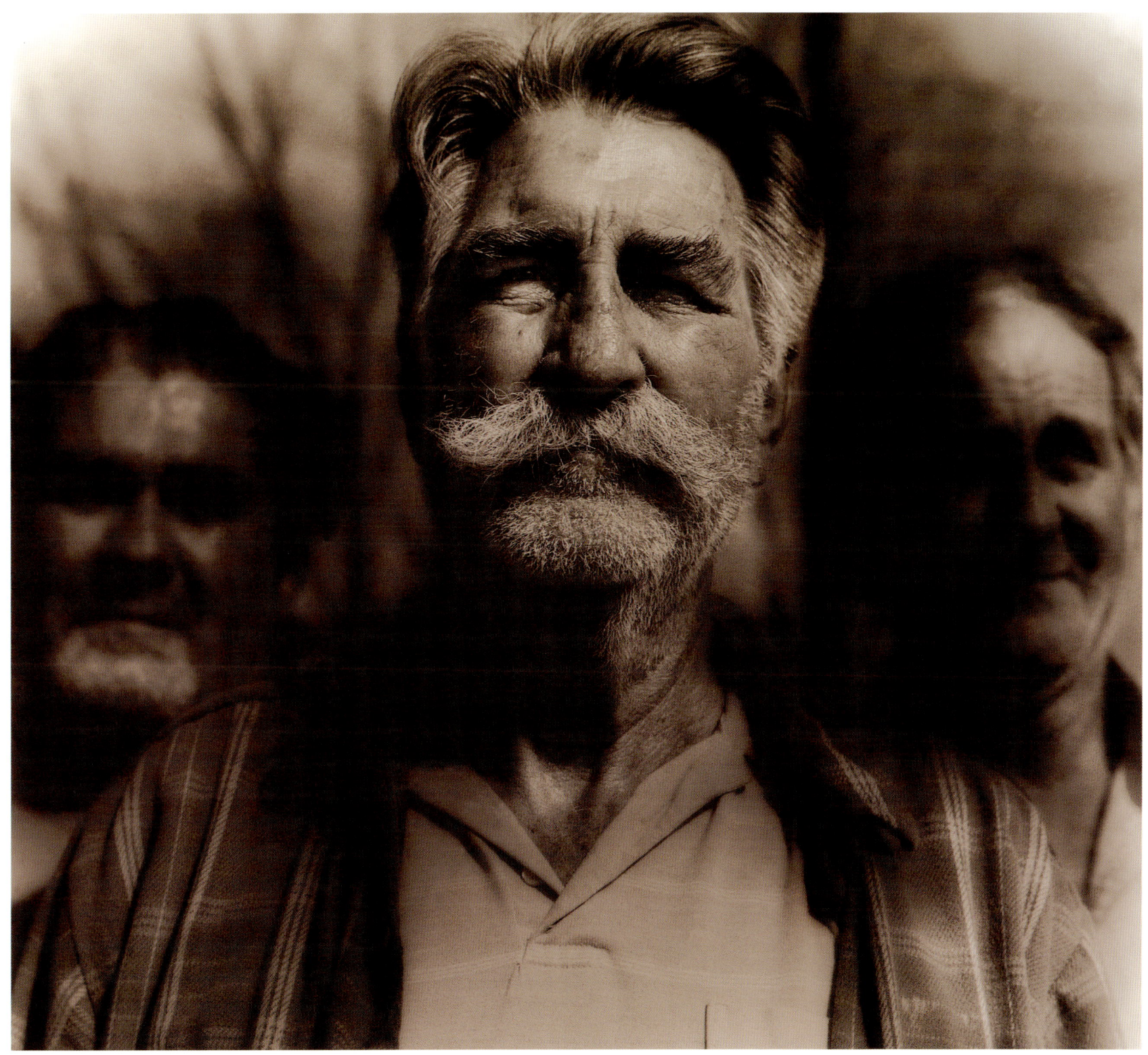

Catfish Boy. 1993, Le Flore County, Miss.

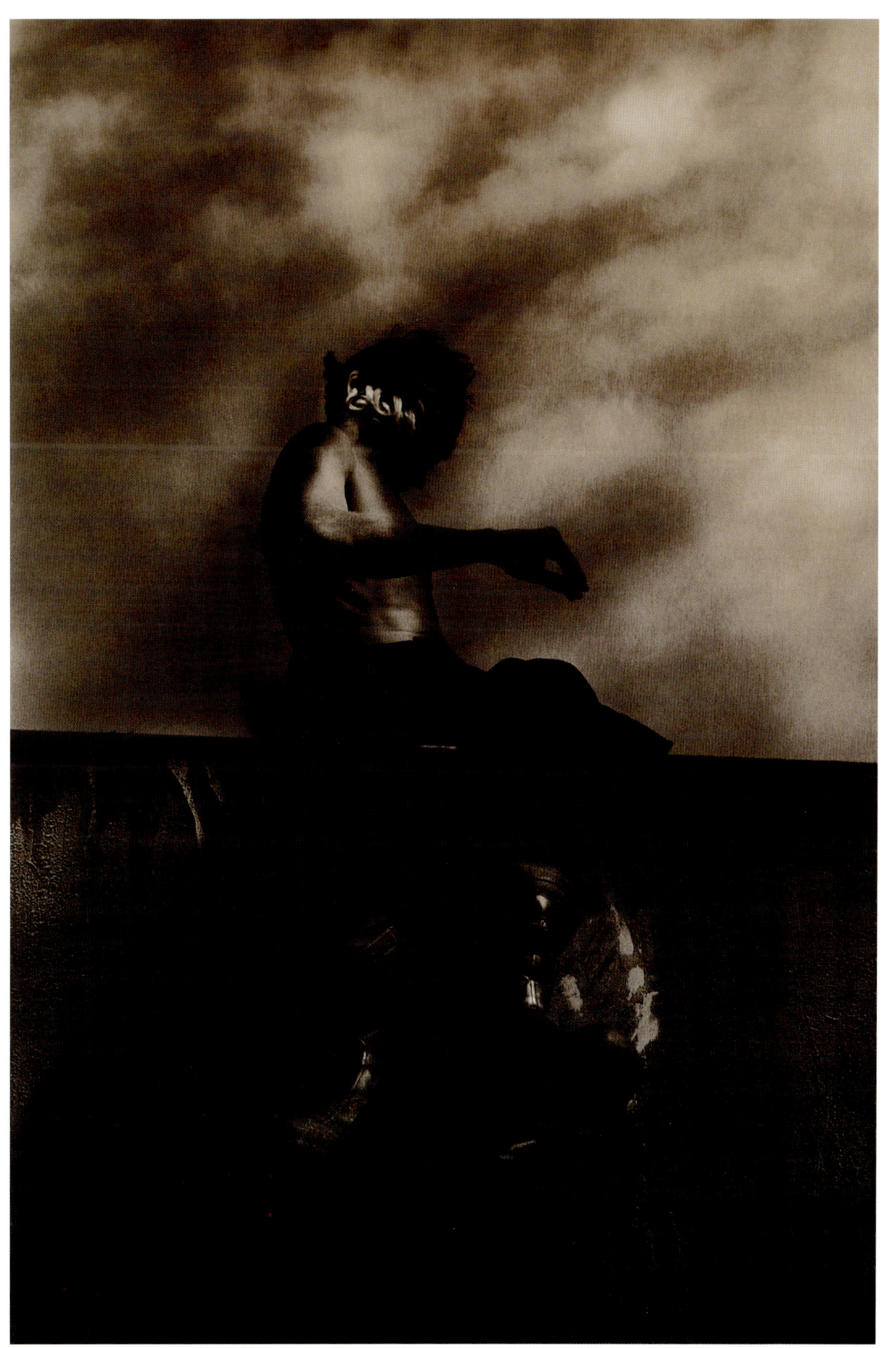

Riders Across the Levee. 1998, Bayou Goula, La.

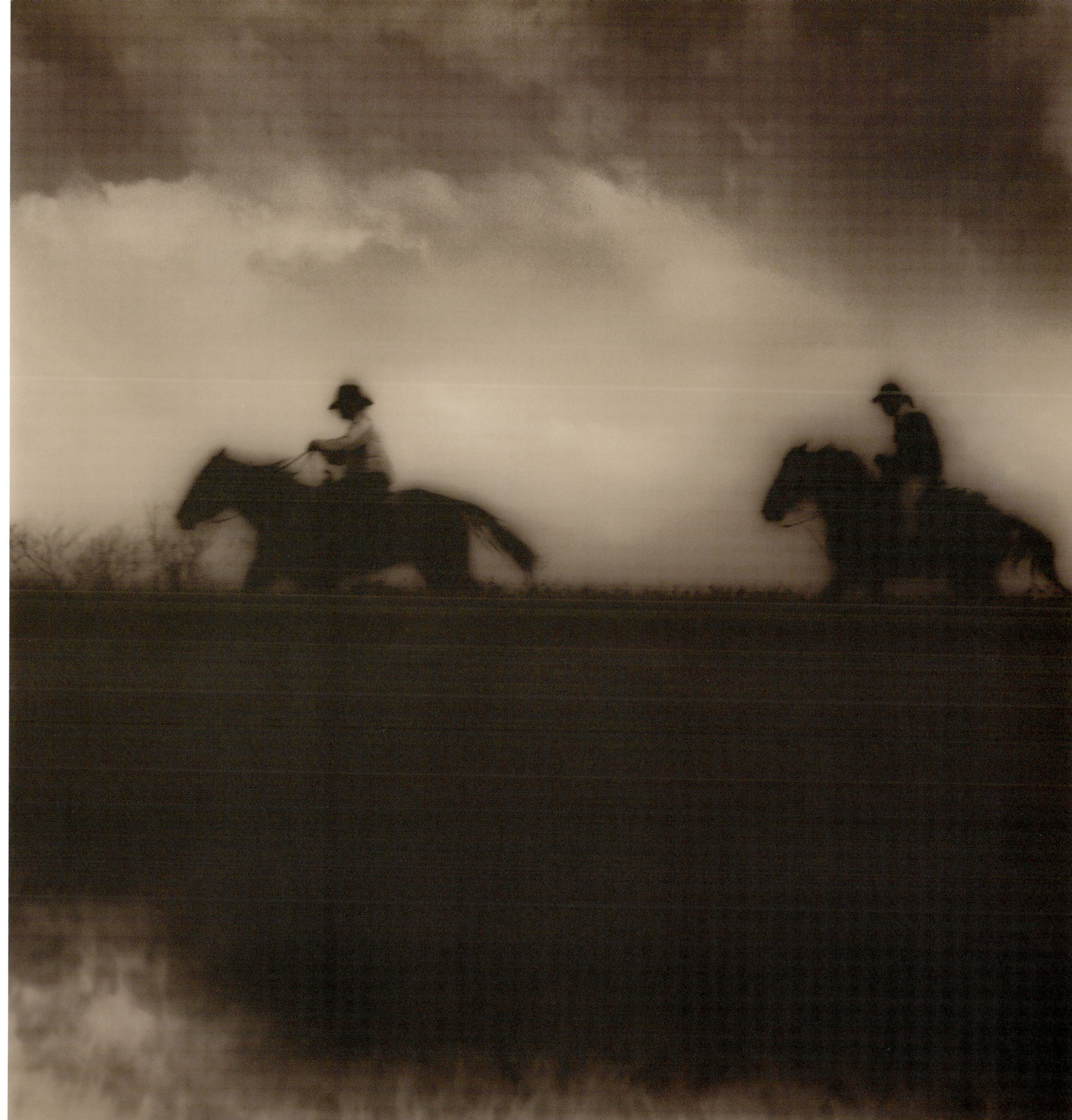

White Horses. 1997, Panola County, Miss.

Fool on a Horse. 1997, Mamou, La.

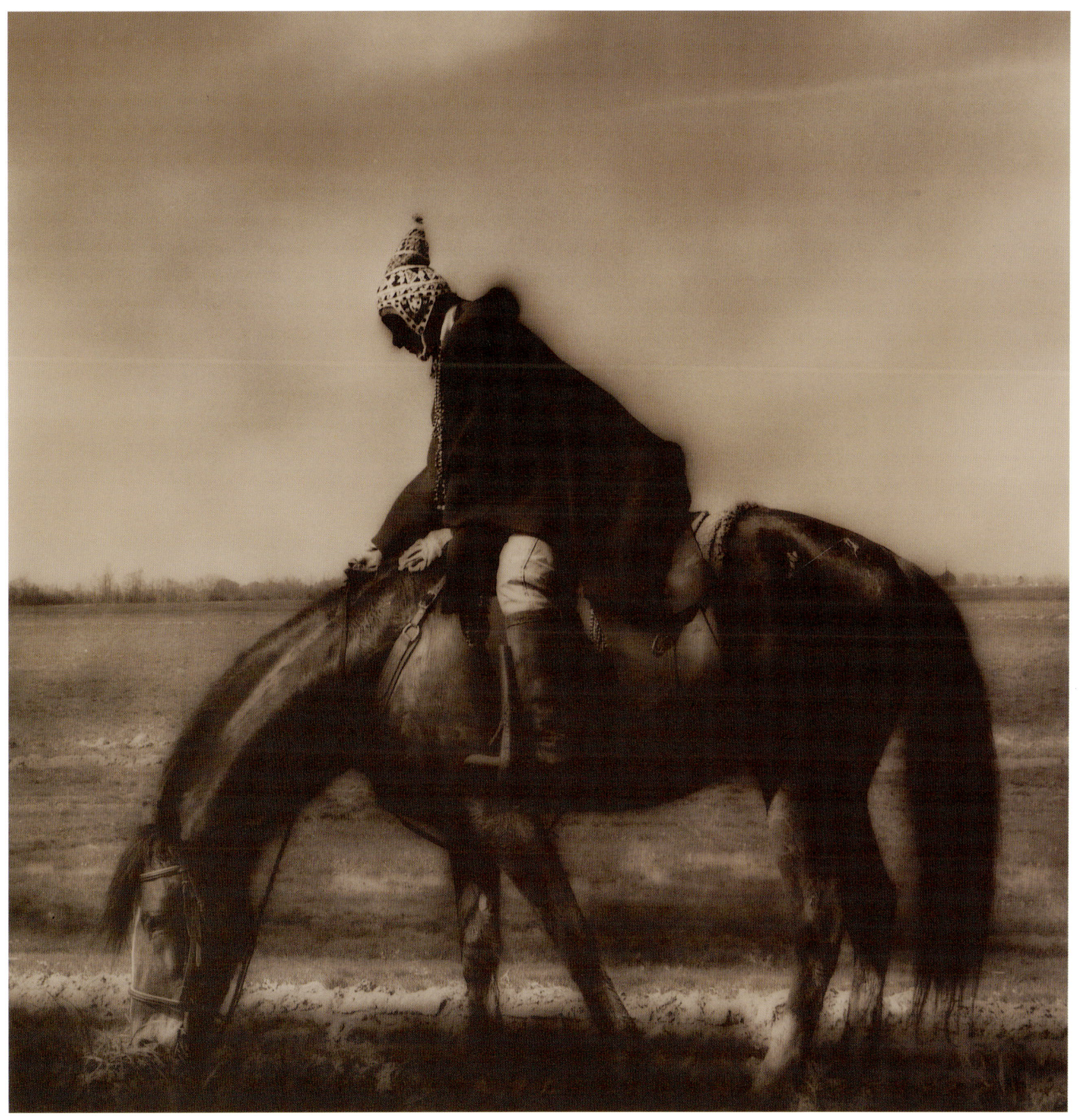

Bull Riders. 1997, Senatobia, Miss.

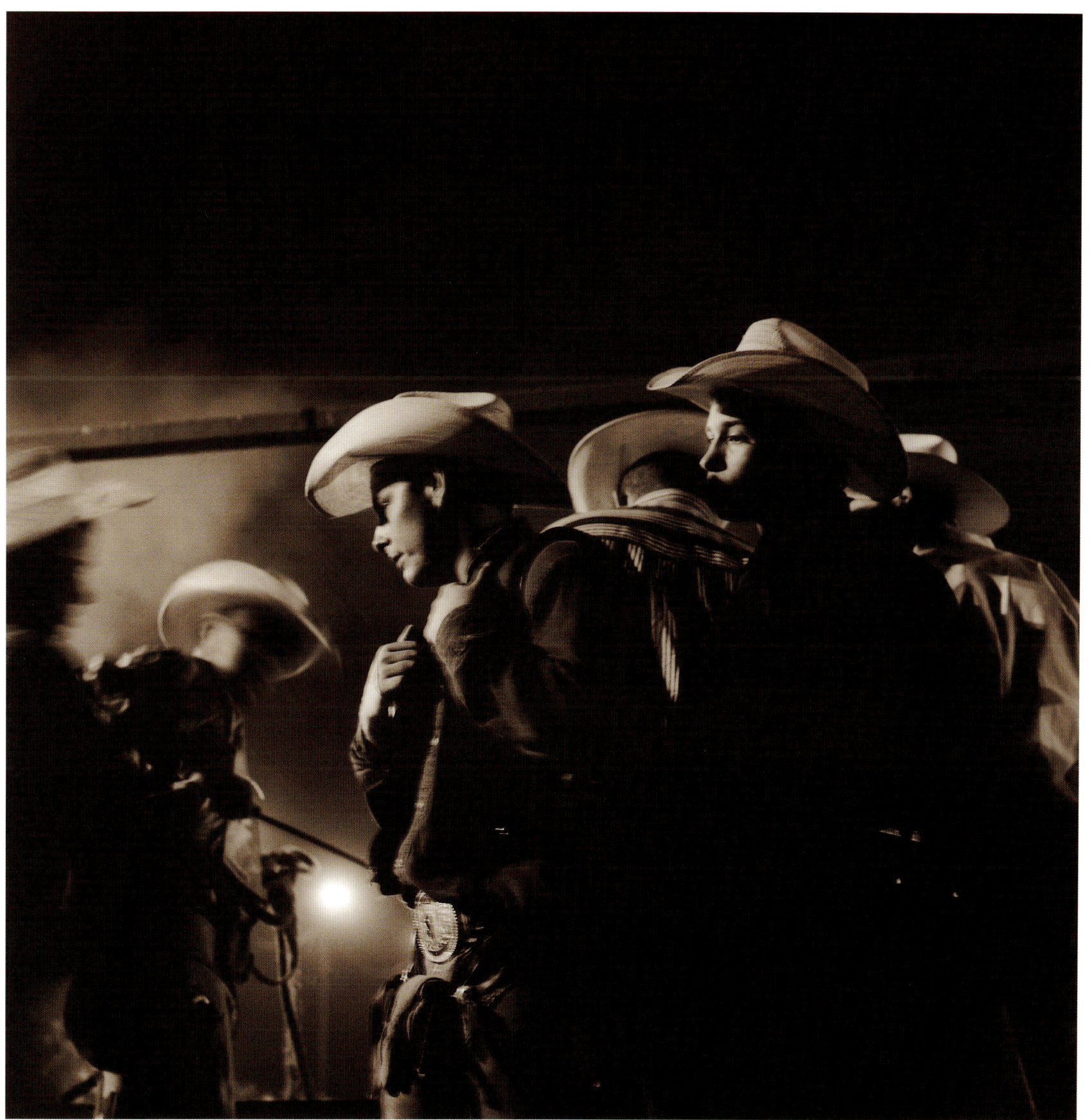

Beast. 1990, Benton, La.

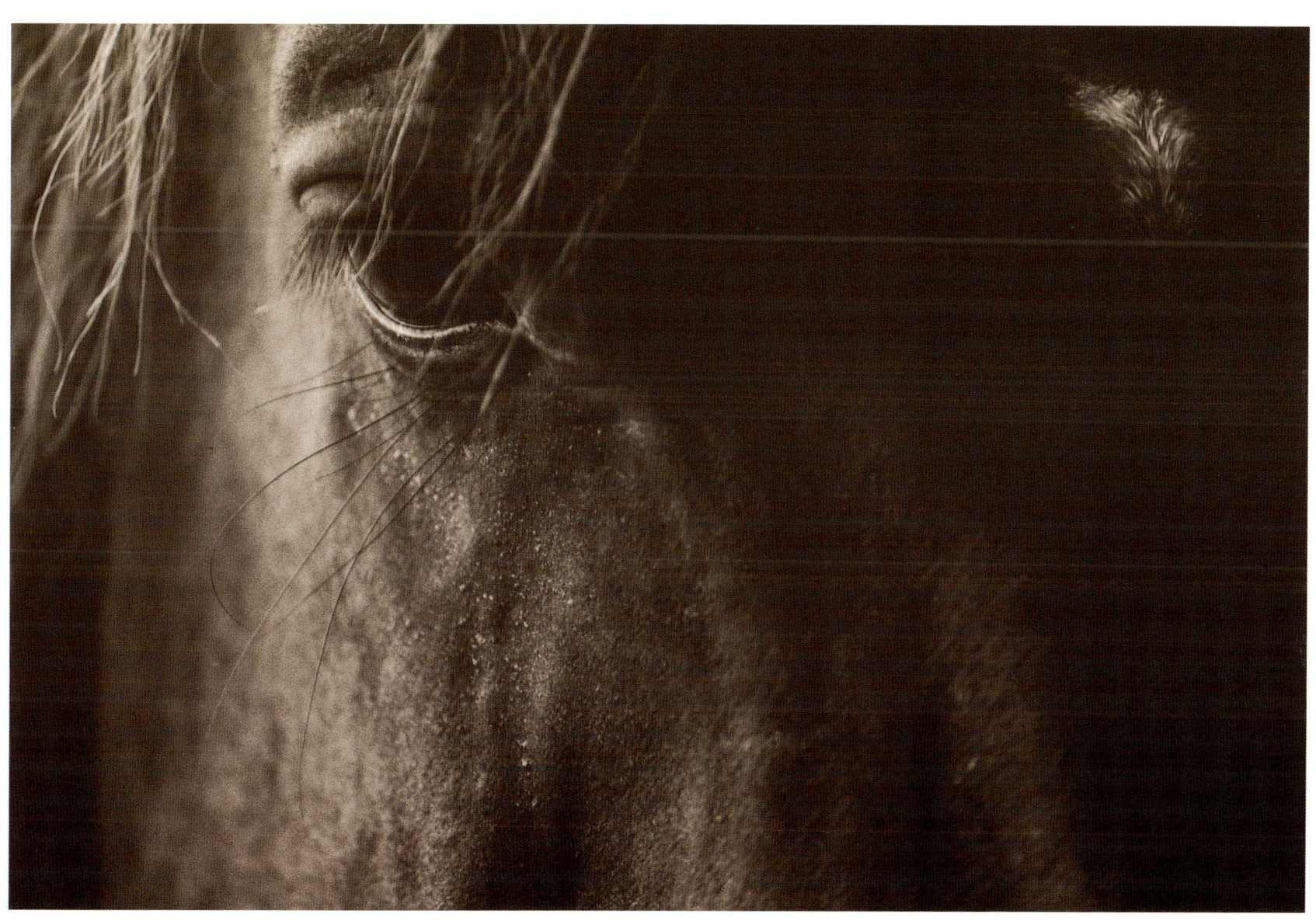

Jimmie's Rooster. 1998, Blackhawk, Miss.

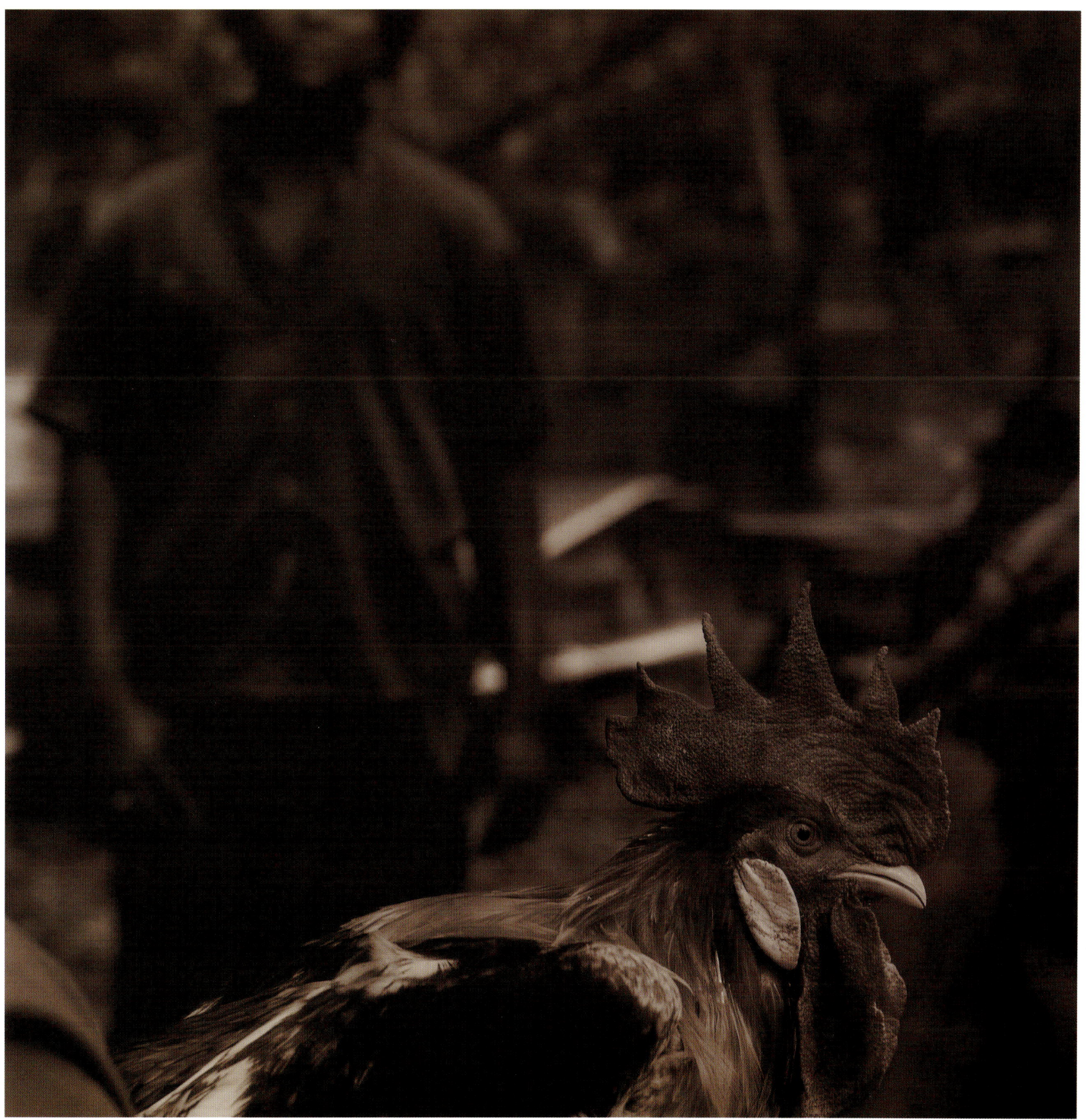

Hellhound. 1991, Estill, Miss.

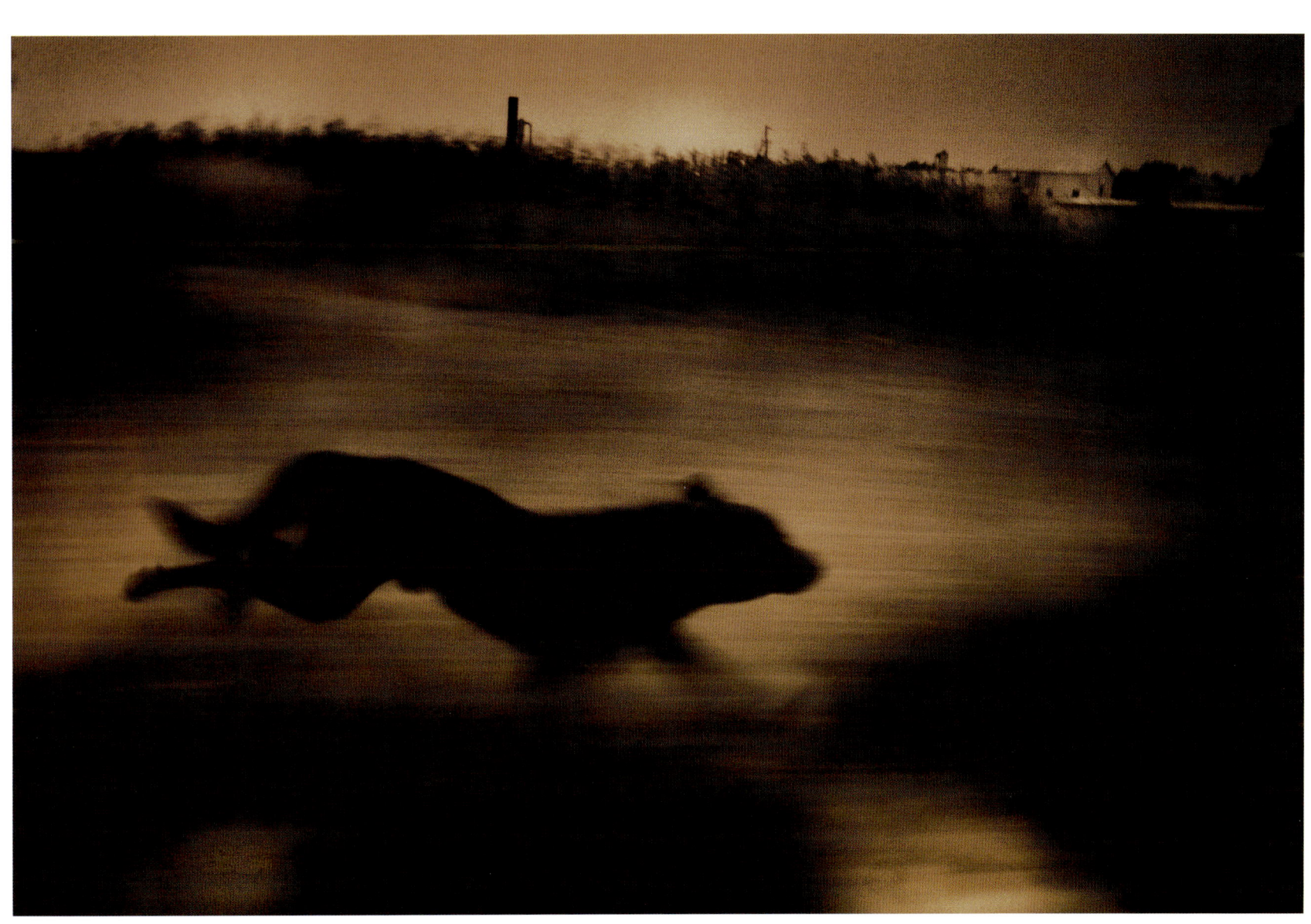

Dominicker Hen. 1994, Coila, Miss.

Overleaf:
Patriot No. 1. 1998, Coila, Miss.
Patriot No. 2. 1998, Coila, Miss.

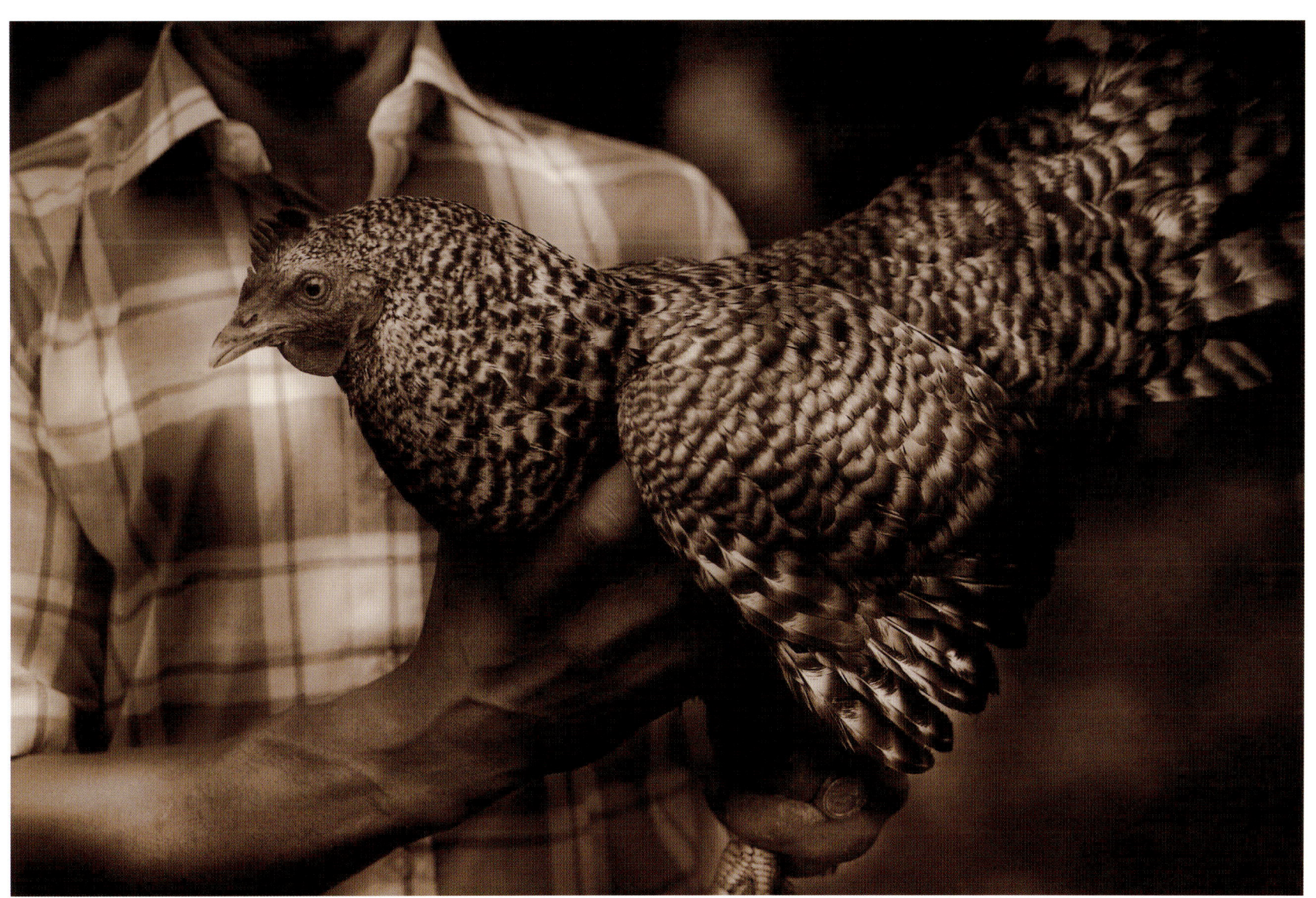

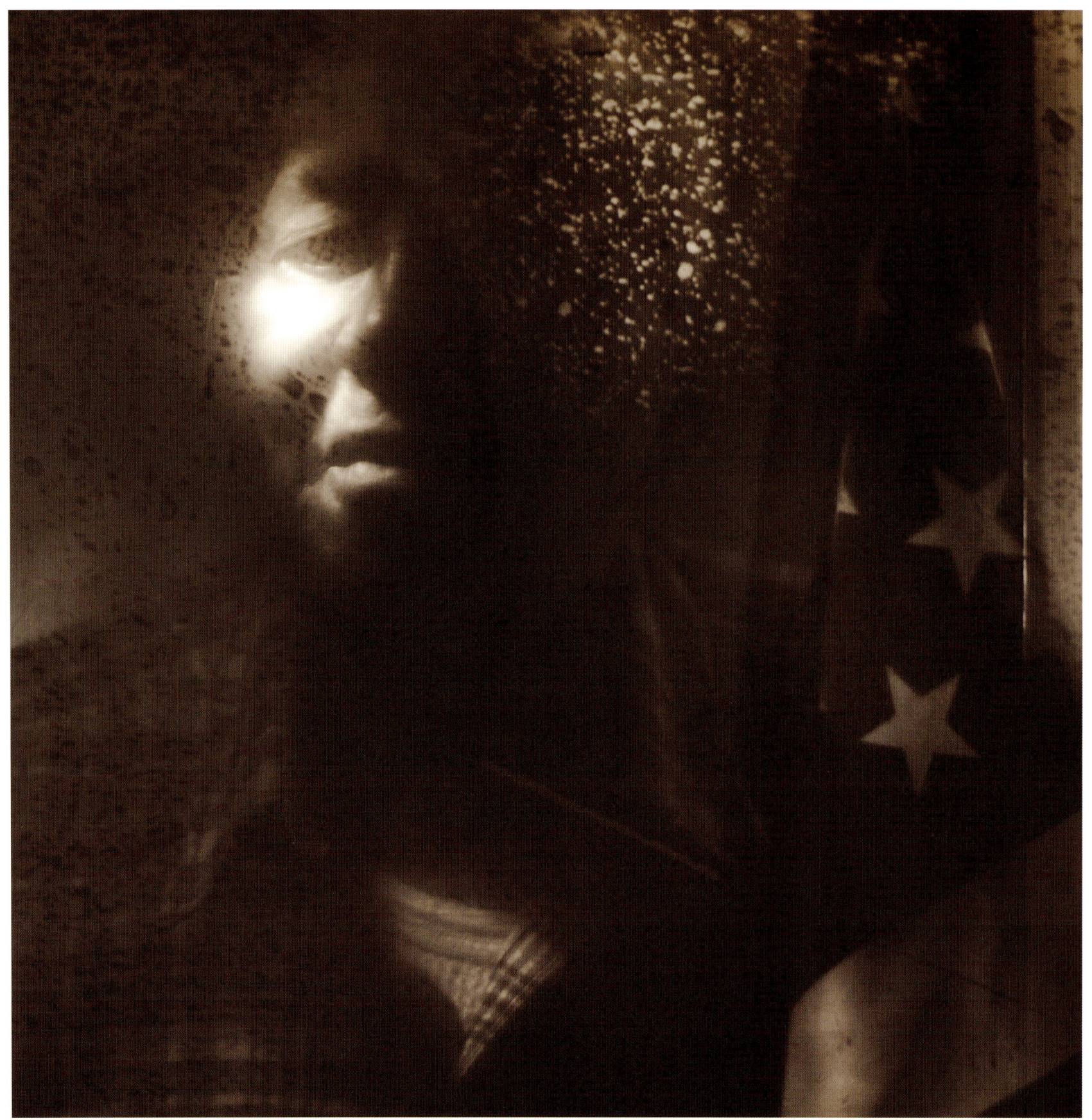

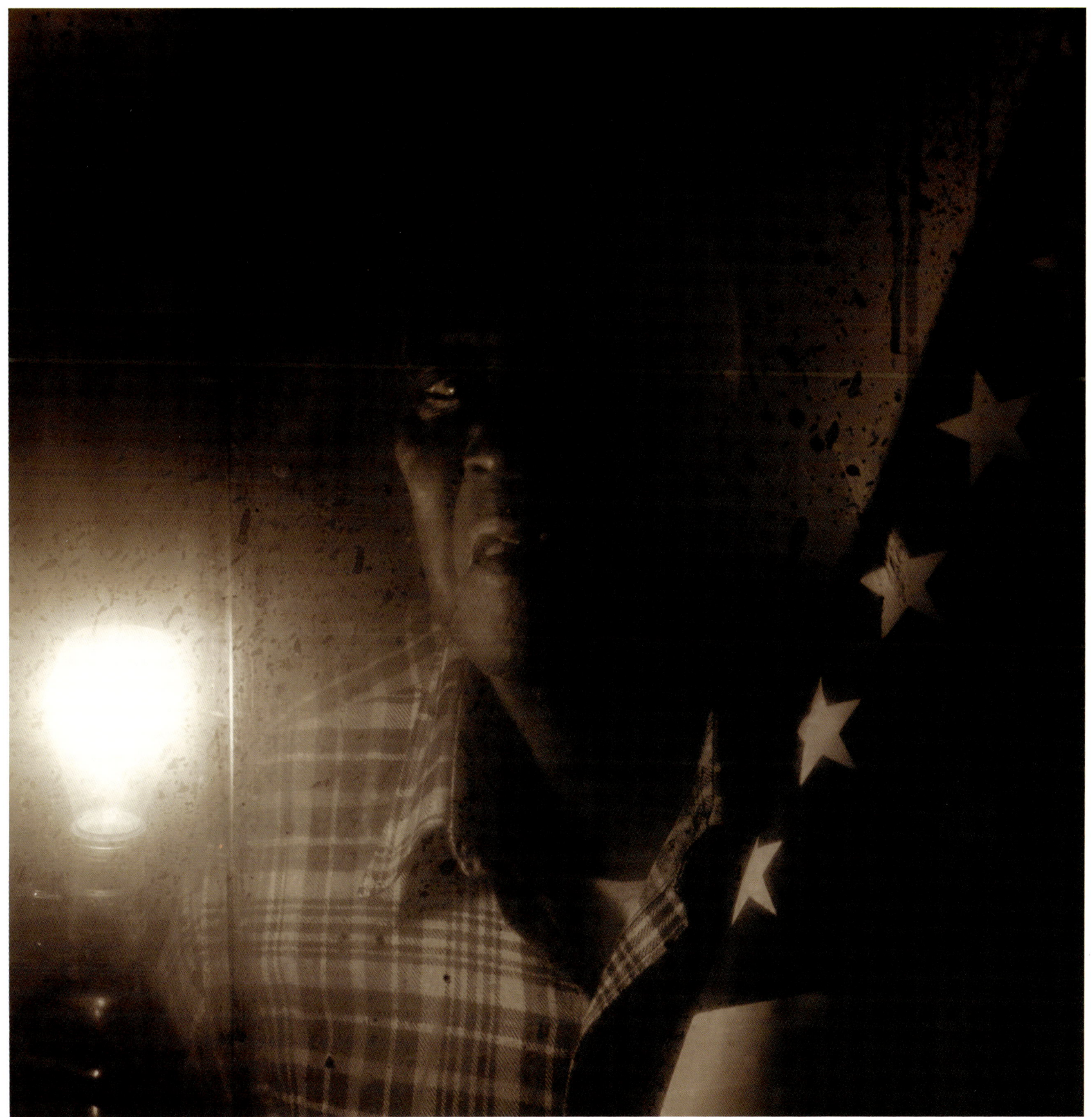

Cooter (Mr. Will Branch) with Glass. 1995, Coila, Miss.

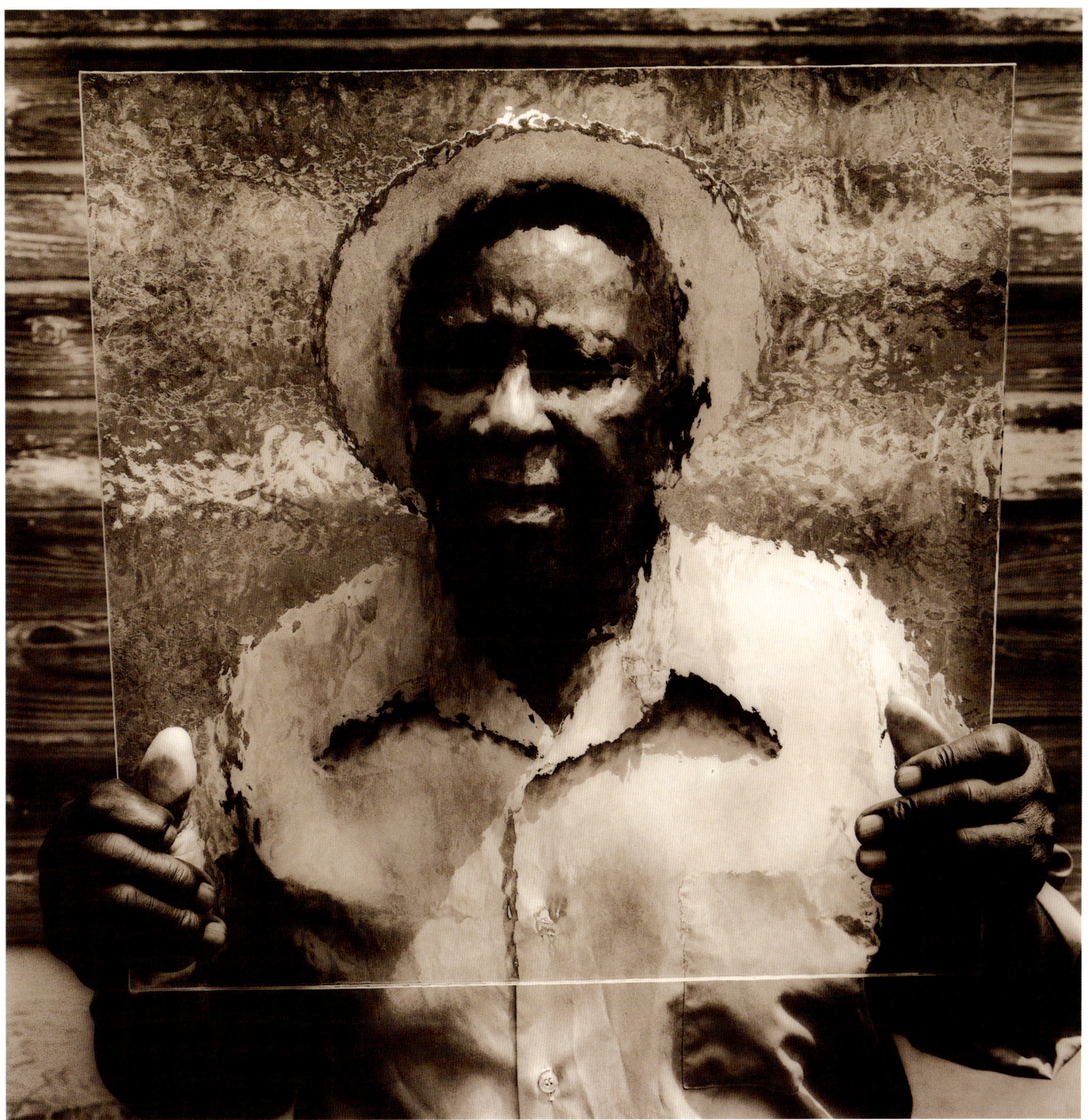

Cooter in the Corn with Horn. 1996, Blackhawk, Miss.

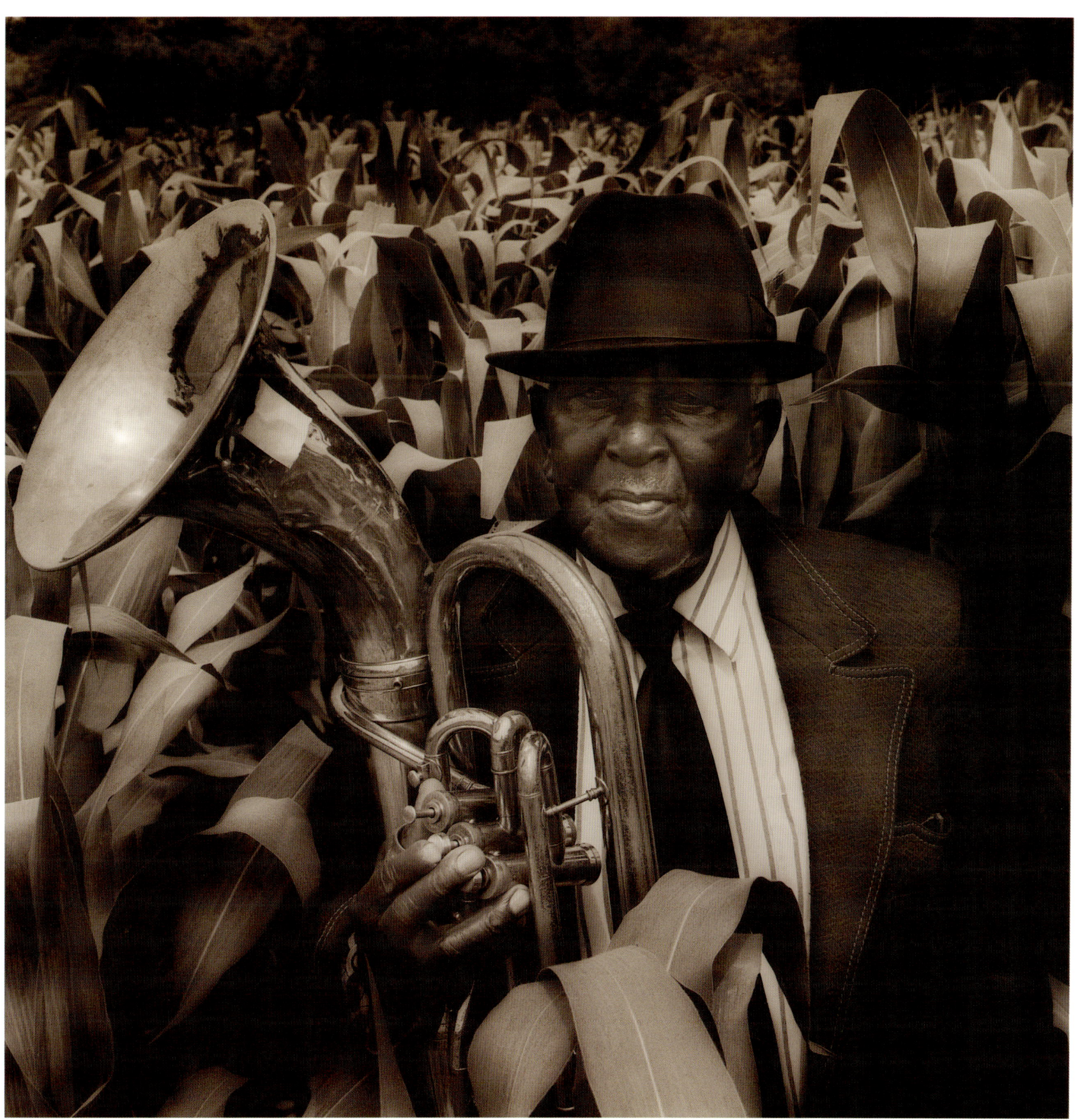

Cowboy Cooter. 1998, Coila, Miss.

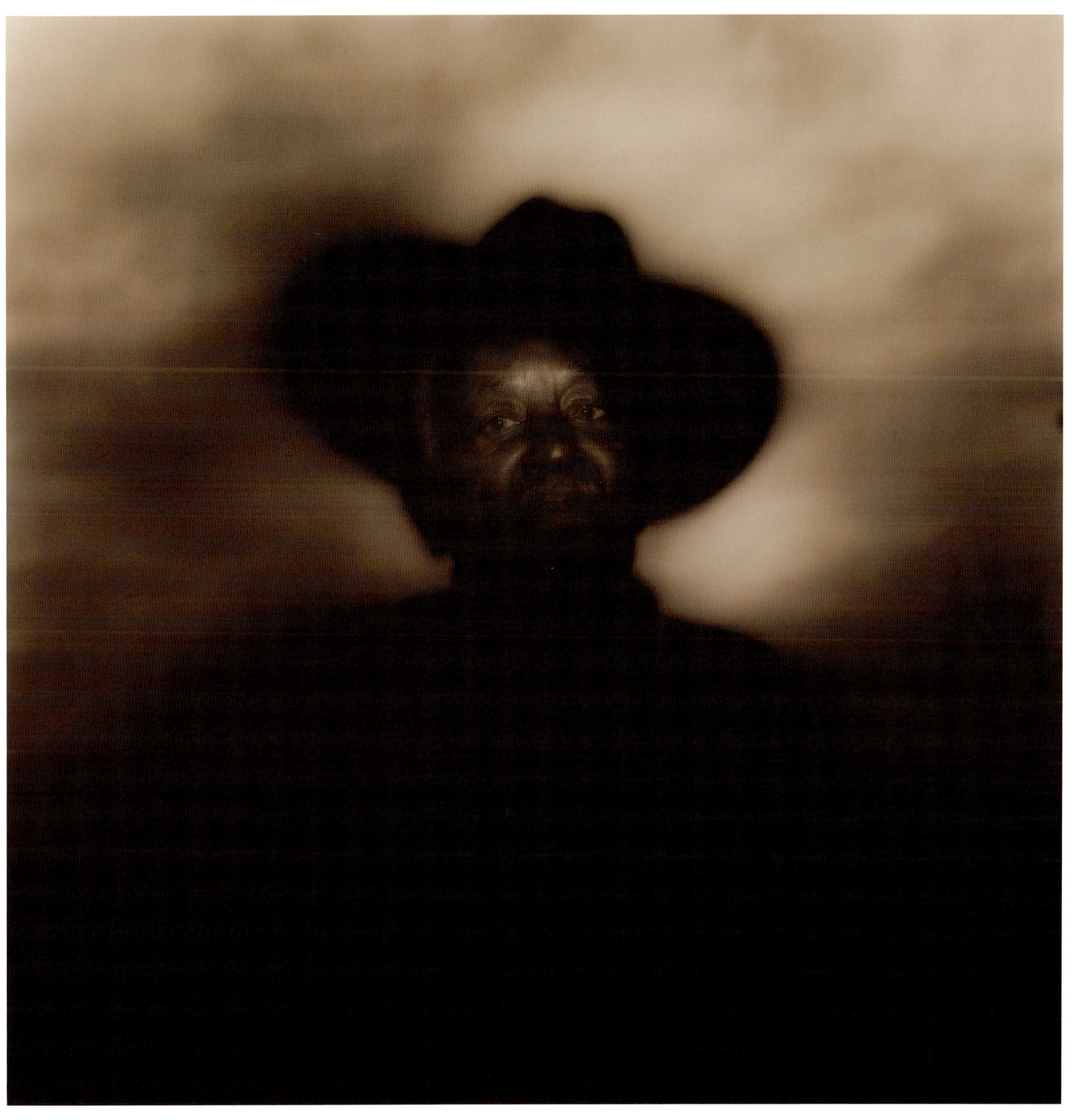

Cooter's Doin's. 1995, Coila, Miss.

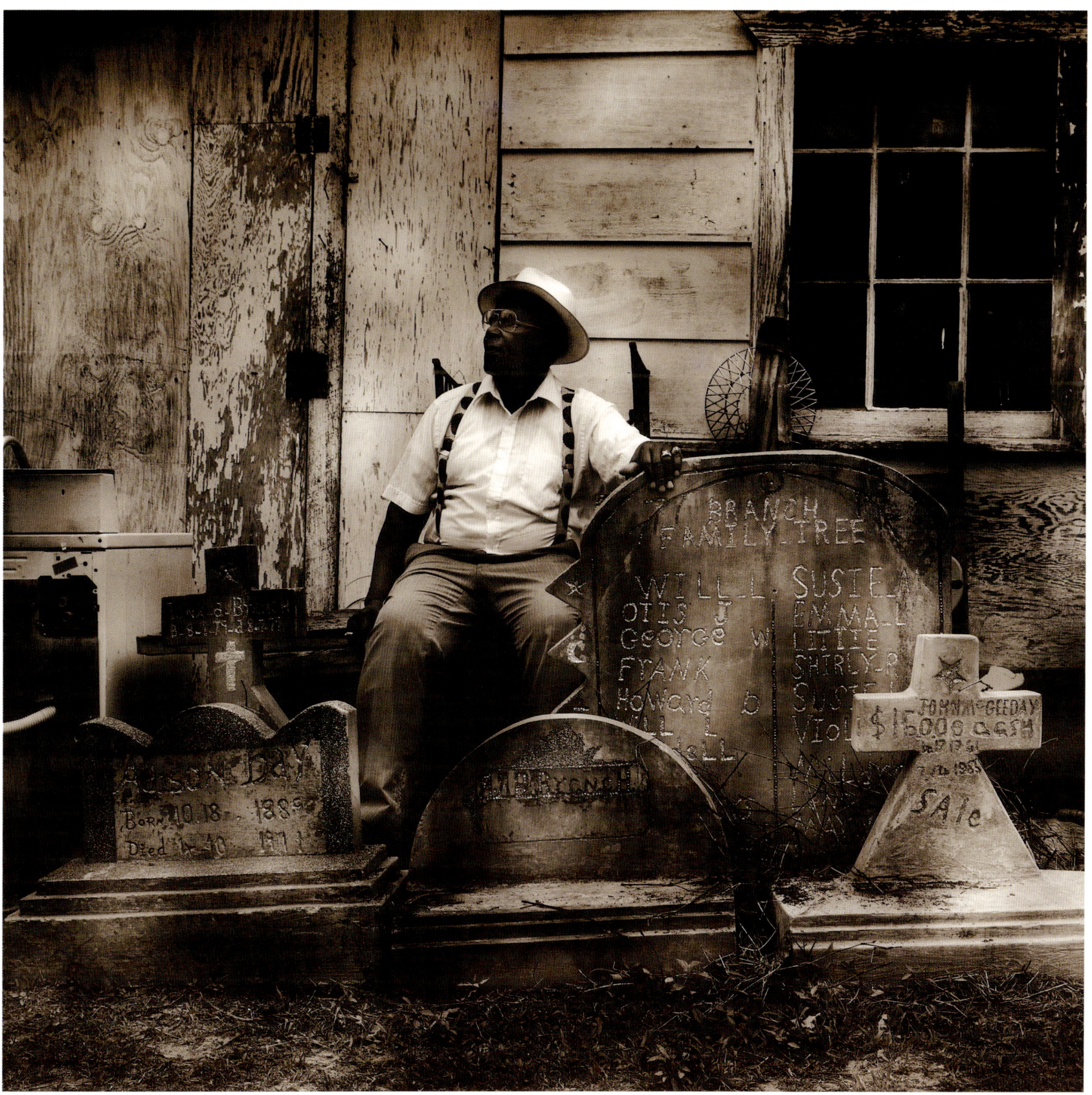

Cooter's Lament. 1994, Blackhawk, Miss.

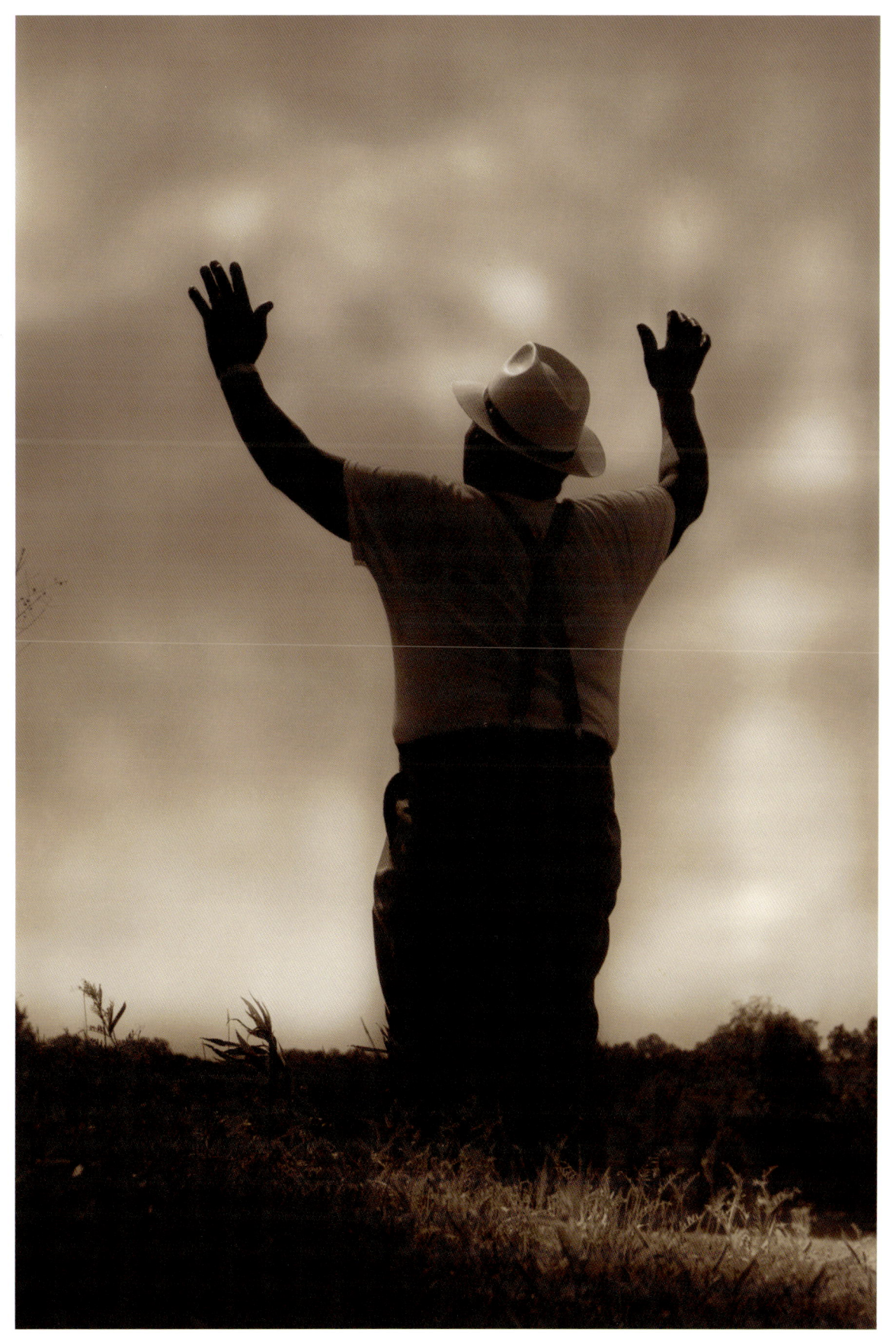

Cooter at the Abyss. 1996, Coila, Miss.

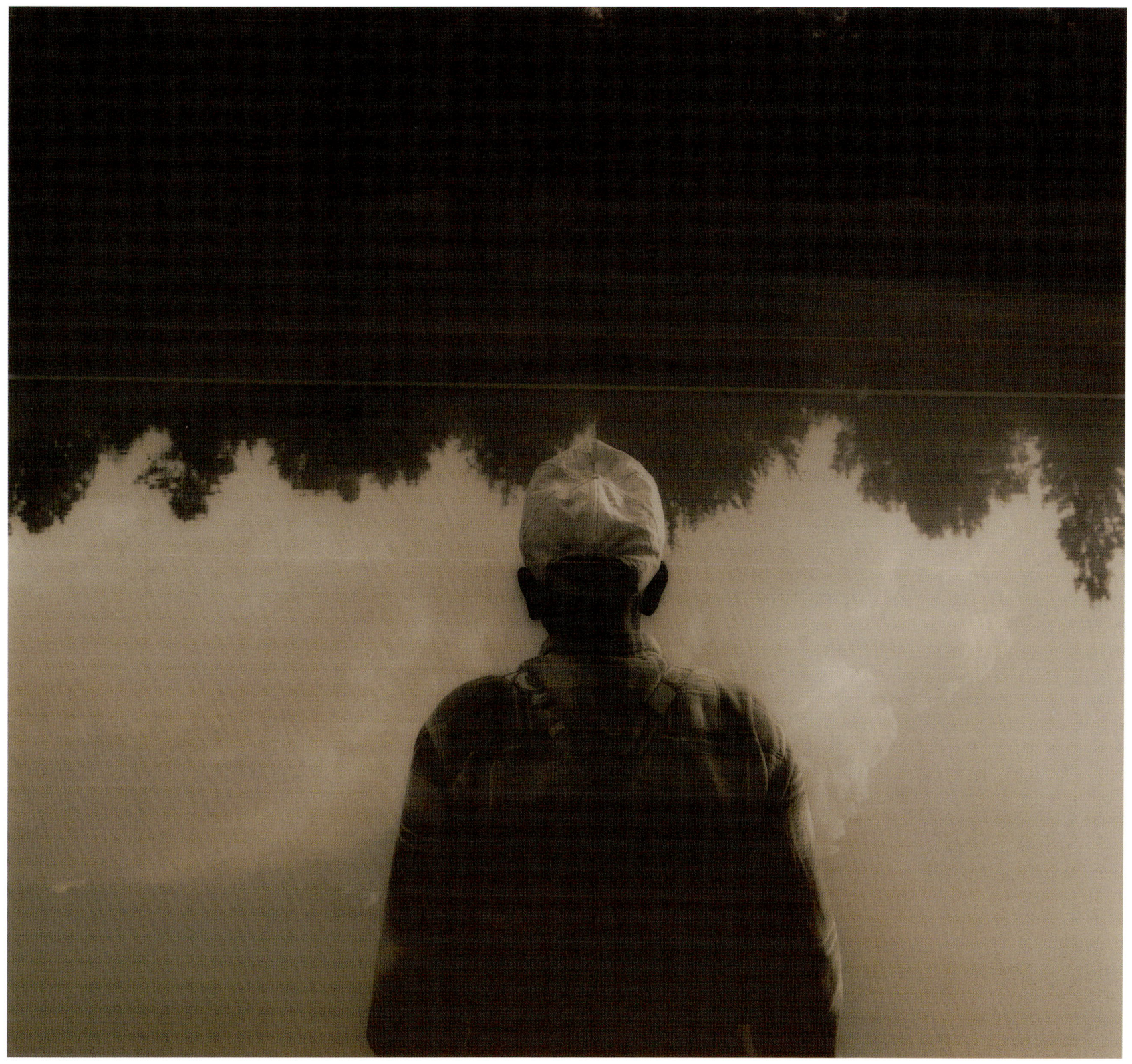

Cooter's Road. 1998, Coila, Miss.

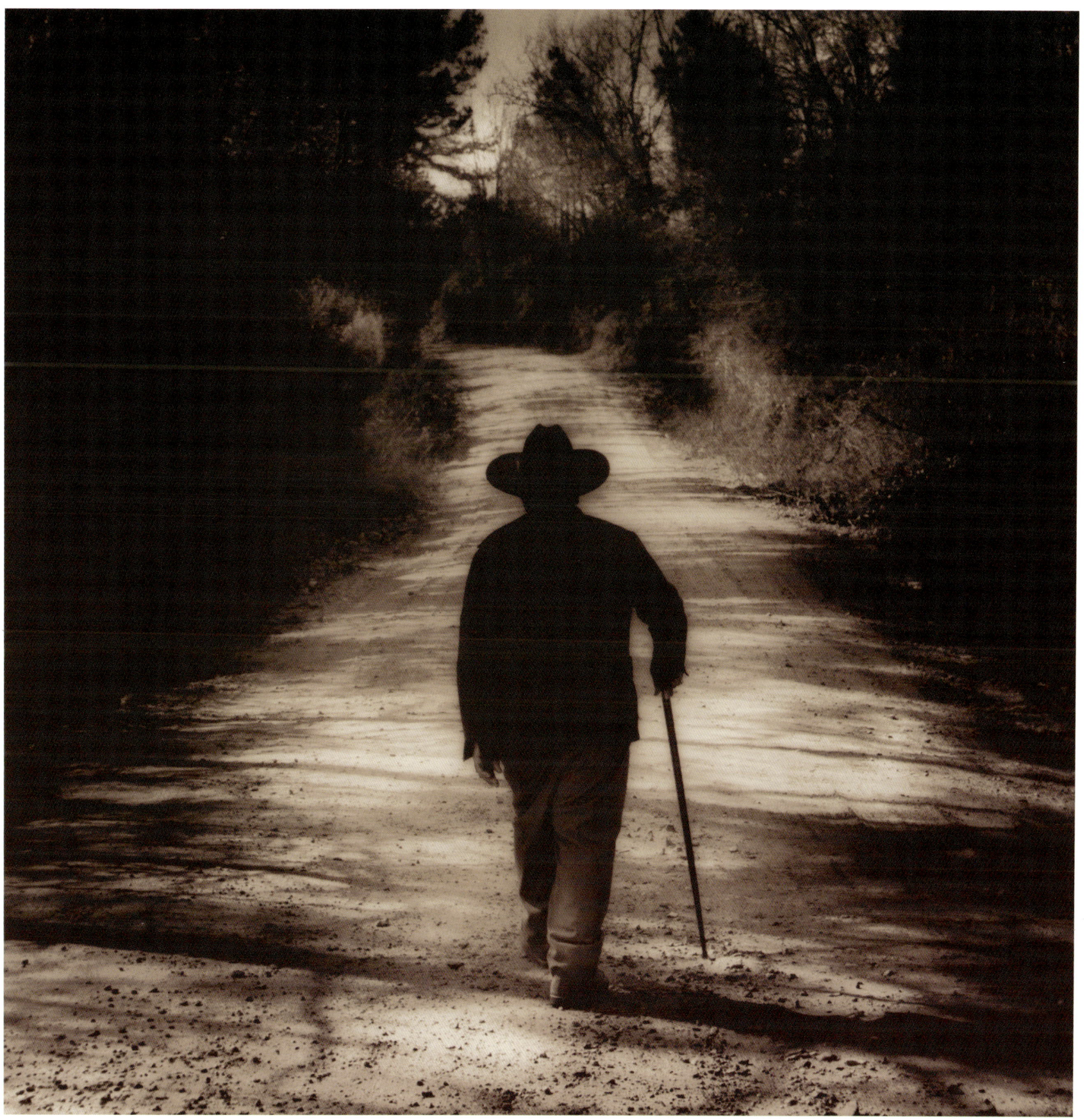

Where you come from is gone, where you thought you were going to never was there, and where you are is no good unless you can get away from it.

—Flannery O'Connor, *Wise Blood*

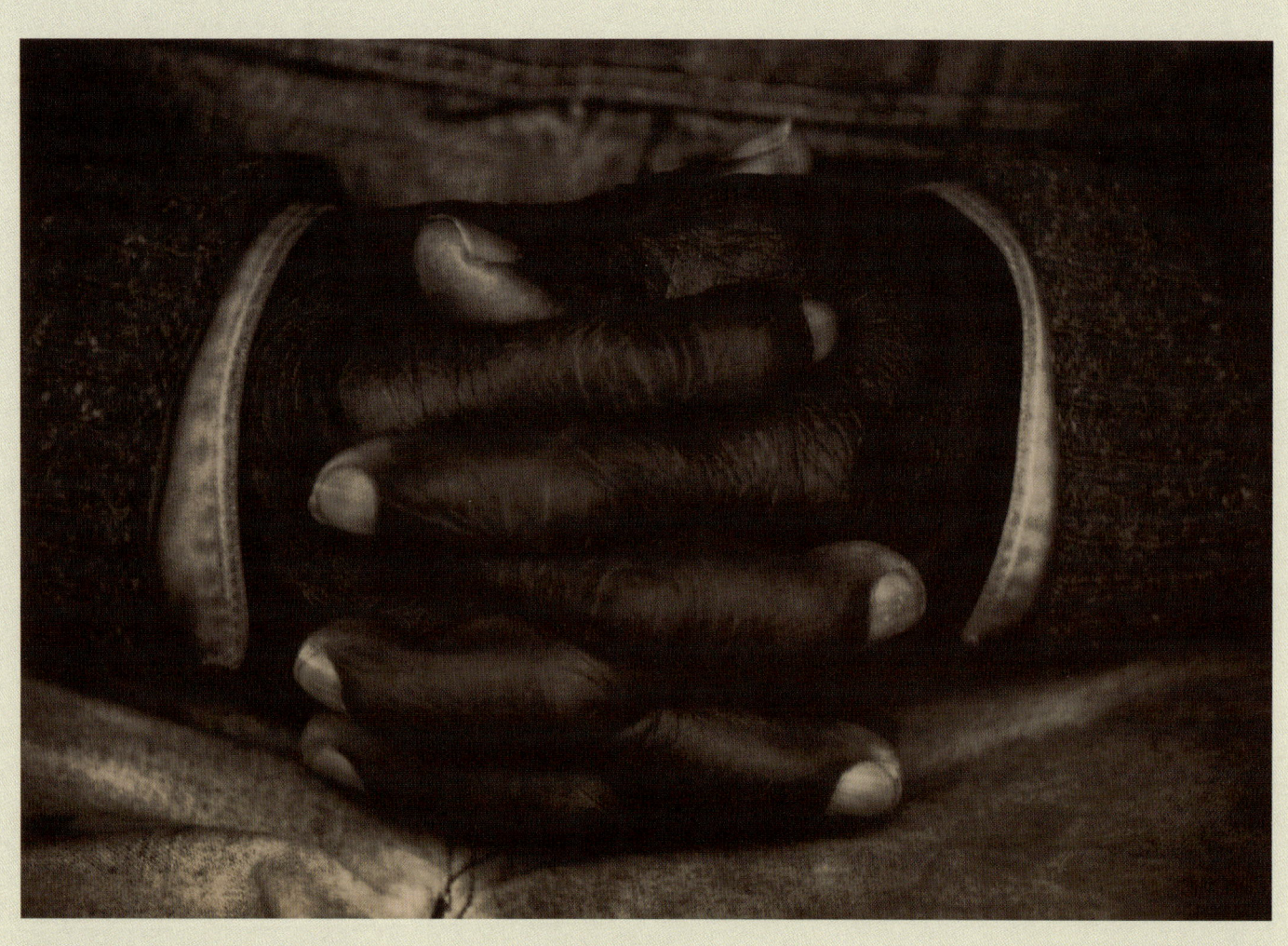

Afterword and Acknowledgments

In my travels taking these photographs, I have been fortunate to meet many fascinating people from all social strata, from the profoundly impoverished to the extremely wealthy—some people deeply content and possessed with joyous spirituality, some deeply mournful, some angry and bitter, and some deliriously, giddily happy.

I met some people who were full of hope and others who it seemed had just given up. Like an old woman I met in Mize, Mississippi, who lived in an absolute hovel. She told me she was "waiting for her death to come," and she did die very soon after my visit. She died not in a hospital, surrounded by attendants, but all alone in that old "piece o' house," as she called it.

Others managed to achieve a kind of sublime transcendence. My friend Mr. Will "Cooter" Branch told me how when he was a young man, his family's farm of a couple hundred acres had simply been "taken away" by some white men. I tried to help him look into it, but it seemed no tracks were left in the public records sixty-odd years after the fact. Such confiscations, I learned, had apparently been a fairly common practice at that time, and nothing could be done about it.

Once I asked Cooter how he felt about white people now. And in his gentle voice he answered: "There are good white people and there are bad white people. There are good black people and bad black people, and God loves them all, and that is what I try to do—love them all."

It has occurred to me, on many occasions during my travels, how truly alike we all are. Down deep, beneath our surface exteriors, behind the masks we all wear, we all want to be accepted, and we want to be loved and treated with kindness and respect.

I think I have been given a gift—a gift of vision. Not just the vision of photography. That is secondary to the vision that allows me to see that every single life is fascinating. I honestly believe that a great novel could be written about each and every one of us. We all have wondrous tales written across our faces. Some are epic, some tragic, some hilarious, some elegiac, and, of course, some are spare, but I believe none would be uninteresting.

Through our struggle, our defeat, our desire and longing, our occasional triumph and transcendence, we are all trying to go home.

So to all you kind souls who, over the years, have allowed me to peek in your windows and witness your tales, I thank you for your wonderful gifts.

There are a number of persons who have been of special help to me in my endeavors relating to this book, and I owe them a great debt of gratitude: Vickie Bassetti, Bonnie Benrubi, Kenneth Blevins, Ann Borum, Wanda Boudreaux, Will Branch, Kristin Bryan, Aubrey Cain, John and Mo Chaisson, Stephen Clark, Patsy Cutillo, Ellen Douglas, the folks at Dury's Pro Shop, John Easterly, Catherine Edelman, Susan Elliot, Gail Gibson, Libba Gillum, Laura Gleason, Laura Grannen, Gary Heard, Debra Heimerdinger, Maureen Hewitt, Patricia Hoefling, David Ingerbretsen, Jane Jackson, Buddy Jones, Sonny Landreth, Marianne Lampshire, Baylor Ledbetter, David Lusk, Karen Marks, Kate Mills, Gussie Morrow, Millie Moorhead, Marcy Nessel, James Patterson, Laura Peterson, Les Phillabaum, Janice Pollard, Claudette Price, Michele Myatt Quinn, William and Ginny Parker, Mickey Raphael, Michael and Lindsay Rhodes, Lea Russo, Josephine Sacabo, Rose Shoshanna, Carol Stein, Melissa Taylor, Claudia Vernia, Anna Walker, Bill Wittliff, Dalt Wonk, and Jamie Wright.

To all of you, thanks, and great big love.

JACK SPENCER